A Man's World

A Man's World

From Boyhood to Manhood 1900-1960

———————— • ————————

Steve Humphries and Pamela Gordon

BBC BOOKS

for my father
S.H.

•

with much love to my dad,
Alan G. Williams
P.G.

•

Page 2: *Young shipbuilders at a launch in 1952. Hard labour carried much status amongst working class youths keen to prove their masculinity.*

•

This book is published to accompany the television series entitled *A Man's World* produced by Stephen Humphries. The associate producer was Pamela Gordon and the executive producer Sam Organ.

Additional research by Sharon Tanton

Published by BBC Books
an imprint of BBC Worldwide Publishing
BBC Worldwide Limited
Woodlands
80 Wood Lane
London W12 OTT

First Published 1996

ISBN: 0 563 37109 9

Set in Bembo
Printed and bound by Butler and Tanner Ltd, Frome and London
Cover printed by Richard Clays Ltd, St Ives plc

Contents

─────────── • ───────────

Acknowledgements

We would like to thank all those who have helped us in writing this book. We are indebted to Sheila Ableman, Anna Ottewill, Frank Phillips, Deirdre O'Day, Sarah Amit, Susan Martineau and Sarah Cartwright of BBC Books for their advice and support. Special thanks to Sam Organ of BBC Bristol for his invaluable contribution to the television series which this book accompanies.

Thanks also to Daniel de Waal, Andy Attenburrow, Steve Haskett, Jeff John, Jan Faull and the staff at the National Film and Television Archive, Tim Exton, Peter Baker, Peter Grimsdale, Julie Richards, all the staff at the BBC Bristol reference library, Madge Reed, Mike Humphries, Rob Perks, Paul Thompson, Mary Parsons, Doris Gibbs, Joan and Val Davies, Norma Jones, Gwen Ling, Bay Gunn, Janet Gillet, Carol Smith, Doreen Hopkins, Marie Crofts, Irene Swift, Doris Gibbs, Christine Page, Barbara Morris, Barbara Robertson, Auriol Robertson, Lily Robertson, Anne Robertson, Isobel de Silver, George, Shirley and Andrew Fowler, Gillian Clements, Irene and Albert Harrison at the Ritz Tea Dance in Manchester, Horsham St Faiths VC First School, The Far East Prisoners of War Association, Norfolk Pensioners' Association, Dragon School in Oxford, Dorchester Record Office, Blackpool Miners' Convalescent Home, Lancashire NUM, Manchester Gay Centre, Jim Soulsby, Life Long Learning University of Central Lancashire, Superintendent Graham Dench, Royal Mission to Deep Sea Fishermen and M and B Charters of North Shields, Phil Woods, Maurice and Mary Pinkney, Dawn Williams, Arts Development Office – Gateshead, Gez Casey, Peter Spafford, Primetime, Lillian Stephenson, Ashley Ramage, Henry and Duncan Barker.

We are, of course, deeply indebted to all the people who spoke to us and whose memories form the core of this book.

Finally we want especially to thank the researchers, David Napthine, Martyn Ives, Steve Grogan and Richard van Emden, whose hard work and determination found most of the interviewees for the series and the book.

Introduction

———————————•———————————

George Ryder is a stocky, well-built man, still quietly proud of the muscles he developed as a young body-building enthusiast before the last war. Liverpool born and bred, he lives on the outskirts of the city in a comfortable, modern bungalow. He is charming, witty and talks very fast. He was brought up in the notoriously tough Scotland Road area and spent much of his working life as a bricklayer. Now seventy-two and a widower, he is very much a man of his generation. His life has been shaped by the ideas of masculinity and gentlemanly conduct that were so influential before the 1950s and that largely dictated what a man had to be and a man had to do. He looks back at the changes since then with a mixture of surprise, bewilderment and sardonic humour.

•

Everything is so different today to the way we were brought up to be towards women. The man was the king pin, he was the breadwinner, he was the provider, but you were always told that a gentleman should always behave properly to a lady. You opened the door. You protected her. You walked on the outside of her. Even today if I walk with a strange lady in the street, like a neighbour, I have to go on the left-hand side of her otherwise I'm uncomfortable. And we were taught to always give up your seat to a lady. Even today on a bus I can't sit while a woman is standing. But I've learned now that I have to sit because when I stood and offered a young girl a seat I've been told to bugger off.

•

George is one of about thirty-five men who we filmed talking about the experience of masculinity for the television series that this book accompanies. These in-depth interviews – here quoted at much greater length – form the core of the book. In compiling this first-person history of masculinity we spoke to or corresponded with about a thousand men born between the 1890s and 1930s. Most wrote to us in answer to our call for memories in local newspapers and on local radio stations. Others we contacted through pensioners' welfare groups, social clubs and gay rights organizations. We have drawn on this material to try to chronicle the most important elements of what it was to be a 'real man' in Britain during the first half of the century.

At that time the demarcation between masculine and feminine behaviour was much more rigid and all-pervasive than it is today. Men enjoyed immense power backed up by an ideology that legitimized their domination. A woman's place was seen to be at home looking after her husband and children and, as a result, they were largely excluded from public life. A 'real man' had a fairly well-defined role as a worker, a lover, a father and – in wartime – a soldier. He was prepared for these adult roles as a boy and proved himself as a young man through various private and public rites of passage. The chapters document manly ambitions and ideals in each of these key areas, and the realities behind them.

There was of course no single, all-encompassing, definition of masculinity. Men's aspirations varied enormously according to their individual circumstances and in particular their social-class background. Personal testimonies reveal a whole spectrum of different ideas about how it was believed a 'real man' should behave. These ranged from chivalrous notions of gentlemanly behaviour fostered by public schools to more predatory ideas of masculinity, deeply rooted in popular culture, which celebrated feats of strength, hard-drinking and sexual conquest. There was rarely any doubt, however, of the fundamental difference in behaviour expected of a man and a woman.

But it was sometimes very hard to be the kind of man most men aspired to be. Behind the ambition to be a 'gentleman' or a 'real man', instilled in boys from a very young age, there were many inner conflicts and contradictions. Male display and pretence often masked the fact that deep down men were often more uncertain and insecure about their roles than they admitted. Danger, fear and physical and emotional pain all had to be endured with a manly fortitude that left some feeling very anxious and alone. Close relationships with women could be difficult for men of this generation. Many felt more comfortable with other men. Yet even in the company of men, few could talk openly about the problems and pressures of being a man. The 'real man' of this era was not supposed to show his feelings let alone talk about them.

In our interviews we have tried to dig beneath the surface and reveal some of the complex, suppressed emotions men did experience.

But getting men of this generation to open up and talk honestly and intimately has not been easy. They are simply not used to talking about themselves and their lives in the way that women are. Women generally tell their stories in a much more personal, moving and revealing way. One of the main criteria in choosing the men who appeared in the television series and the book was their emotional honesty and their willingness to think and talk about subjects which might frighten many older men off. Their testimony provides a vivid document of the experience of masculinity in the recent past. Precisely how representative or typical it is has to remain a matter of conjecture – there are just too many silences to say with certainty. However, their stories are not just a matter of historical record. They also help shed a little light on male attitudes today. For despite the fundamental changes in the position of women since the 1950s, and the demise of the 'gentlemanly ideal', some of the old ideas of manliness and masculinity have proved remarkably resilient and remain very influential today. Many contemporary social problems and gender issues such as male violence, discrimination against women at work, the absent father and the sexual double-standard clearly have deep roots in the 'man's world' of the first half of the century.

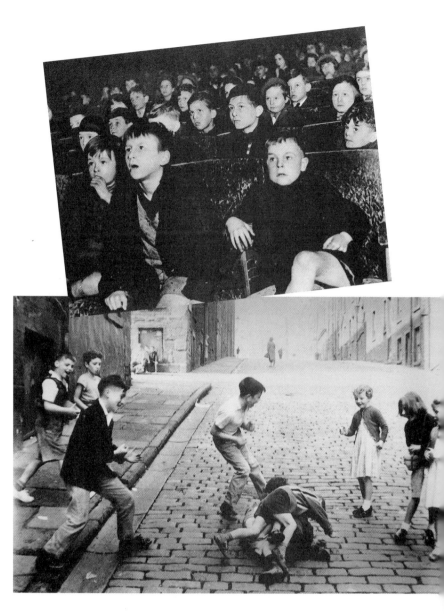

Top: *Boys engrossed in a cinema show in the 1940s. The rigid taboos of the time prevented boys from showing their emotions, the cinema being one place where they could let them run free.*

Above: *A gang of boys in an Edinburgh street in the 1950s. The pecking order of the street culture was based on strength and the ability to fight.*

•

CHAPTER ONE

The Boy

———————— • ————————

Dave Bowman, the son of a railwayman, was brought up in Dundee in the 1920s. One of his abiding memories of the rough and tumble of a Scottish boyhood is that 'it was sissy to cry. I didn't cry, for a boy to cry it was considered a weakness. When you got the strap, your hand was stinging for a week but you didn't cry. We had a concrete playground and we played football there and of course we'd short pants, so if you tumbled over your knee would get very badly scratched but no one ever cried. If you cried, everyone thought you were a weakling, it wasn't just a question of strength, it was a question of strength of character.'

Perhaps the most striking feature of the remembered world of boyhood in the first half of the century is the shame of shedding tears. Men recall how girls would cry – that was natural – but for boys it was unusual, and the worst insult was to be called a sissy or cry baby. A stiff upper lip, instilled in some boys from the cradle, was especially pronounced in men who are now in their eighties and nineties. The extraordinary repression of feeling that this stoicism induced in them as children was revealed time and again in their stories, and most vividly expressed when they were confronted by the grown-up world of suffering and tragedy. Geordie Todd, the son of a shopkeeper in North Shields on Tyneside, dearly loved his mother but could find no tears to express his emotions when she died in 1920. 'I wanted to cry but I couldn't, I just had this big lump in my throat, no tears. At the funeral me sisters was all crying but I think I just stood there stone-faced.'

Men of this generation – whatever their background – saw themselves, in their young days, as utterly different to girls. At home they remember different rules of behaviour for boys and girls. Some were encouraged to think of themselves as 'little gentlemen' who should always be a credit to themselves and their family. Tony Kildwick, brought up in a well-to-do Yorkshire family in the 1920s, eloquently describes some of the pressures of such a training in gentlemanly conduct, with parents who were virtual strangers to him and the miseries of a boarding-school education.

The rigid demarcation of roles was most dramatically expressed in middle-class homes when at the age of around eight boys were sent to boarding-school. The trauma of suddenly leaving home and being removed from the care and company of women – sisters, mother and nanny (sometimes the most sadly missed of all) – remains deeply etched in the memories of older middle-class men. It was particularly distressing for nine-year-old Alec Gunn as it coincided with the separation of his mother and father: 'I had a very happy childhood really, it was a privileged childhood, and then quite suddenly in this black September of 1928 it all collapsed in a cloud of smoke. My father walked out, my beloved dog Torchy who was a little mongrel terrier was put to sleep, my nanny was sacked and I was packed off to boarding-school and all this happened in about a week.'

There were separate spheres, too, for the majority of boys and girls who stayed at home. Most went to sex-segregated schools. Even in mixed schools they normally sat on different sides of the classroom, had separate playgrounds divided by high walls or fences, and were treated differently by teachers. Practically all clubs and organized play for children, the most popular of which was the Boy Scout and the Girl Guide movement, strove to keep boys and girls apart. It was a division that was largely unquestioned. Not surprisingly, when left to their own devices in the streets and fields, boys and girls rarely played together. A serious friendship between a boy and girl was almost unthinkable. Dave Bowman recalls his childhood in Scotland in the 1920s, 'the boys were always on their own and the girls were always on their own. Childhood was boys for boys, and girls for girls, and never the twain shall meet.'

During the first half of the century it was widely assumed that boys and girls should be brought up in a different way to prepare them for the very different roles they would have to play in adult life. Generations of schoolmasters, scout leaders, churchmen, brigade captains and mission workers – many from a public school background – were inspired by an ideal of boyhood they wanted to instil in boys from all classes of society. The boy should be plucky, courageous, courteous, respectful, sporty, sporting and, perhaps most of all, patriotic. This was an era when there was immense pride in Britain and her Empire and it seemed an admirable calling to train boys to be

Top: *Boys playing leapfrog in a London school playground in the early 1900s. Such games were an important part of working-class children's culture, yet sex segregation meant that boys and girls rarely played together.*

Above: *A bout at a boys' boxing club in the 1930s. Boxing was considered important training for manhood for young boys of all social classes.*

•

Boys join a patriotic march through London at the outbreak of war in 1914. Young boys, fed on a diet of imperialism and heroism, were caught up in the wave of jingoism which swept the nation.

•

upright citizens, disciplined workers and brave soldiers. These efforts to shape the character of the boy were, in part, driven by a Victorian ideal of manliness, rooted in the public schools and the neo-Spartan virility of cold showers, stiff upper lips and playing the game. The ideal of Christian manliness was epitomized and popularized in *Tom Brown's Schooldays* by Thomas Hughes. It became the forerunner of a new genre of such boarding-school stories.

Stirring adventures and heroic ideals had much appeal for boys, especially the notion that Britain was a great nation whose sons had a noble duty to bear arms. George Short grew up in a mining village in Durham in the 1900s: 'I started school in 1905 and we were always reminded that we were the superior race, we were the race which owned an Empire on which the sun never set. We really believed that. And we would be playing games of soldiers, everybody would make his own sword, get a stick and put a cross on top of it, and like knights of old we would be fencing. One side would be the British and the other side would be the Germans, and of course everybody wanted to be on the side of the British 'cos we were the ones that had to win.'

The few boys who dared question the flag-waving jingoism before and during the First World War were ridiculed and ostracized, as is movingly described by a 'conchie boy' Alfred Jenkins, born in 1903 and brought up in a pacifist family in Neath.

Amongst the middle classes psychological demands were made on boys from a young age. Memories of boarding-school life before the last war reveal the terrible loneliness and anxiety suffered by boys trapped in these spartan and regimented institutions. In 1929 at twelve Humphrey Gillett was sent to the City of London Freemen's School as a boarder. 'It was terrible to be suddenly in a strange environment with masses of boys. I was in the sick bay with a high temperature and I got out of bed and smashed the windows with my fists so I must have had a lot of deep psychological trouble.'

In an era when a boy's status depended more than anything else on his prowess on the games field, those who had no interest or aptitude for sport sometimes found school life difficult and humiliating. The obsession with sporting achievement in both private and state schools could be especially upsetting for disabled boys like David Swift who grew up in Nottingham in the 1930s and 1940s.

Elementary schools were generally harsh and brutal in the way they shaped the character of working-class boys into a disciplined mould. Canings – often for the most petty offences such as poor handwriting or talking in class – were an everyday occurrence. Boys seem to have been punished with greater frequency and violence than girls. Most were too frightened to tell their parents for fear of getting another beating at home. But the canings occasionally provoked angry protests from parents. Joe Phillips, born in 1927 and one of a family of thirteen, was brought up in the only black family in the mining village of Senghenydd in South Wales. 'It was near sadism, any infraction of the rules and you were caned. I was once caned for swaggering when I was marching, I didn't even know what swaggering was. But if I got caned and told my father, if he thought it was unjust then he'd be up the school and if he thought there was any prejudice in it whatsoever he would go to town on the teacher. Once he did have the teacher by the scruff of the neck and it took two or three teachers to hold him back and they threatened him with prosecution.'

Very little classroom violence was recorded in the school log or punishment book. It was not in the interests of schools to document behaviour by teachers, pupils and parents which could damage a school's reputation. This was especially true of school strikes staged by the children themselves, which headmasters were always keen to deny had ever happened. It is only through living memory that they can be properly recorded. There was a nationwide strike in September 1911 involving hundreds of schools in which the boys downed pens and marched through the streets demanding the abolition of corporal punishment. (There were few girls involved.)

It was started by the boys of Bigyn School in Llanelli, South Wales, and the majority of strikers who came out in sympathy in the following weeks were boys. The strike was quickly crushed but there were other sporadic, local protests like the one in 1923 by the boys of Horsham St Faith's village school in Norfolk, vividly remembered by Wilf Page who helped organize the strike. Interestingly the school log-book makes no reference to the strike at all.

Schools, scouts' brigades, church lads' clubs and mission halls had only moderate success in inculcating discipline and the duty to authority in working-class boys. They never tamed the wild and anarchic elements of their culture – especially the gangs of boys in poorer areas who spent their free time on the streets, These boys admired physical strength and courage, ritually tested in individual fist fights and territorial battles with neighbouring areas. Although these were the qualities that reformers like Baden-Powell, founder of the Boy Scout movement, also admired and tried to build on, the more anti-social features of the working-class boys – the swearing, bad manners, hostility to adults and lack of respect for property – all proved impossible for adult authority to eradicate. This street culture is amusingly remembered by Frank Davies, brought up in Salford, the 'classic slum', in the 1920s and 1930s. Books, art and music, he recalls, were viewed by fathers and sons as effeminate and embarrassing.

It was working-class boys who invariably got into trouble with the law and the difference between the sexes was also apparent here too. In the 1930s only one girl was prosecuted for every thirteen boys. During the last war child crime rates soared by almost 50 per cent between 1939 and 1941. Danny Slattery, a boy in South London during the Blitz, describes in shocking detail how the war provided new opportunities for vandalism and theft. His lack of any patriotic duty or sentiment graphically reveals the limits of the campaign to inspire street-wise working-class boys with public-school ideals of Christian manliness. Poverty and class were just too big a barrier to overcome.

Alfred Jenkins

•

Alfred is a sprightly ninety-two-year old. He has lived alone since his wife died, and now looks after himself in a bungalow just outside Wrexham. He became a Labour councillor in 1949, a position he kept for nineteen years. Years of public service have made him a very well-known and respected local figure. He was born in 1903 near Newport, South Wales. His father worked in the sheet mill department of the tin plate works. He was brought up with three brothers and four sisters. Both his parents were members of the Independent Labour Party and were pacifists. Alfred remembers the effect a pacifist upbringing had on his childhood and family during the First World War.

•

We didn't have any guns as children to play with, because my father and mother were dead against anything of that kind.

Alfred Jenkins in 1916 aged thirteen. During the First World War his family was ostracized by the local community in Neath because of their pacifist beliefs.

•

Nor toy soldiers, I never had any. My father and mother wouldn't have bought them for me, no question at all. They were opposed to violence before ever the war took place. And they were opposed to bullying but they always taught me that I would have to stand up for myself. They were peace-loving people, pacifists and they felt very strongly that they didn't want to encourage their children to play at being at war.

There used to be discussions in the house, my parents and friends of theirs who were members of the ILP (Independent Labour Party) used to come to discuss Labour Party policy, socialism. I remember in my early days I'd be sitting there and I'd be absorbing a lot of it. It wasn't a case of children being seen and not heard, I mean, we could be there when they were talking with other people and we weren't told to shut up. We weren't part of it but we were there.

When the war broke out I was then eleven years of age so I knew what was going on and my father and mother had a very rough time. They were ostracized because they were not prepared just to sit back and say, 'Oh I'm opposed to the war.' They tried to do something about it. The jingoism in those days had to be seen to be believed. Everybody was waving flags and rushing to join up. But there was a movement going that was opposed to the war, fostered by the Independent Labour Party, an anti-war movement and they believed in peace by negotiation. They were pointing out to everyone that the slaughtering of one another wasn't a solution to a problem. My father and mother were the only socialists and the only people opposed to the war in the street. They attended the peace meetings and put large window bills in the window of the house advertising these particular meetings. So we became known as Jenkins the

Conchies. They referred to us as cowards, the implication being that we were afraid.

So I was the target of the other boys, partly as a conchie boy and partly because when we moved to Neath in South Wales, we only came from Abertillery which was about forty-five miles away, but we were regarded as foreigners. They liked to hear me talking, see, in order that they could poke fun at my accent. They'd try and get me talking and try to aggravate me so it didn't make life pleasant for me.

I was ridiculed more than attacked. I had my back to the wall kind of thing and they'd say, 'Yah conchies' and all that kind of thing. And of course I was greatly outnumbered. I naturally more or less reflected the views of my parents and I suffered a certain amount of victimization as a result of it. I did feel sometimes, 'Why have we got to be so different. Why aren't my father and mother like everyone else?' My life would have been easier and then after I would probably criticize myself for losing my faith in them and feel a bit guilty about it.

Now my elder brother, he was only sixteen and he joined the Army. I remember him coming home one night standing at the bottom of the stairs and he shouted up, 'I'm off Dad.'

'Off where?'

'I've joined the army.'

It was a tremendous shock for my mother and father but he had come under the influence of the men he was working with and a whole gang of them had joined up. My father told him not to step foot in the house again. He cut himself entirely to fight. It didn't change their opinion of the war, in fact, I think it hardened them a bit. But they were always waiting for a letter from him. When he came home they received a card from the War Office saying he'd been wounded and he was sent to hospital at Caerphilly. They went to see him as soon as they could.

It was a question of principle, not cowardice or anything like that, 'cos my father was far from a coward. My mother was determined, far from being a coward, she knew that she was ostracized to a certain extent but she would still insist on putting that bill up in the window. Well, what happened on one occasion when we had the bill in the window advertising a peace meeting on the common we got up in the morning and my mother went to the front door, and the windowpane where the bill was posted was all smeared with human excreta. The front door, the brass fittings had been smeared with it as well and the letter-box and the doorstep. I remember my mother's revulsion and disgust when she opened the door that morning, you know and found what they'd done.

I was proud of my parents, proud of my father, proud of my mother. It would have been easy for them to have gone the way of the crowd. To fight against the wind was hard going, to fight against the prevailing school of thought must have been very hard for them, but I'm proud, now, today to say they stuck it.

Wilf Page

•

Wilf is a big Norfolk man, a pipesmoker. When he stands he seems to fill the front room of the tiny cottage he shares with his wife, Christine, just outside Cromer. He is a natural storyteller, able to talk with authority and entertain for hours. Politics have dominated his life and, now, in his eighty-second year he is very involved in the pensioners' movement. He is vice-chairman of the National Pensioners' Convention and chairman of Norfolk Pensioners' Association. Wilf remembers his first experience of protest when he and his fellow school-boys went on strike at the village school in Horsham St Faith's, Norfolk, in 1923.

•

You'd be caned for almost anything that you did, if you were late going to school in the mornings or if you didn't get back after playtime when you should be back, or if you made a noise in class you weren't taking the attention that the master thought you should take. I certainly got plenty of caning.

They had these canes the girls dance with you know, these kind of dancing things. The master used to cut them in half so that he'd got a nice curved cane to hit you with and he'd leave them in his office and get one out when he wanted one. If he left one on his desk one of the boys would be bound to pinch it in break-time and we used to hide them in the back of the piano. I know after a while the old piano didn't work so they had to get the piano tuner in to have a look and there were all these canes rolled out.

But we had one woman teacher and she was a very kind teacher

Wilf Page aged nine with his family in 1922.

•

and it was very seldom you had kind teachers in those days. She used to tell us little stories and that sort of thing, playtimes. We enjoyed listening to her so much and so she had no need to cane us. In fact, when we used to get the cane, quite often she'd creep up and try and soothe us and calm us down and show sympathy towards us. We used to sometimes go into the playground and try and ease our fingers and she would come along with you and just pat you on the back as if to say you know, don't worry, you'll get over it sort of thing and it was a wonderful atmosphere.

And then it was just about a month before we were due to break up for the summer holidays, we were informed that she'd got to leave school and not come back in the following term because she was just about to get married. Women in those days could only work up until they got married, then they had to give up their job.

So we thought, well, we're not having this, and about three or four of us got together, most of the boys over ten and decided we'd go on strike to get her back the next term. We insisted on not having any boy under eight years because we thought that was too young to go on strike and we wouldn't have any girls with us because we thought it was not a girl's place to go on strike.

We were out for several days. We all got a stick each and we marched up and down the road with a handkerchief on the top of it. Our parents knew we were on strike and they were very unhappy about it and they wanted us to go back to school. But we sat up in the horse pasture for several hours in the day, talking about things and wondering whether we were doing right and wondering whether we were going to get our teacher back.

Then on this Thursday, Harry Leadbeatter the headmaster, was at the school gate as we marched past and shouted, 'Now I want you all back and we'll have a friendly discussion about what the problems are and see if we can get it sorted out.' But we just walked past him and went up to the horse pasture, had some kind of pow-wow kind of discussion anyway and we decided that we weren't going to go back because he wanted us back but we'd go back when we thought it. So we marched back again and he was still there and we said, 'We'll come back on Monday'. That gave another day's strike for us. And on the Monday morning we all went in and there was a policeman in there and the local magistrate, bloke by the name of Spurrell, and headmaster called some of us boys out and he picked out about six of us. I was one of them who was called out and he caned us, we got two vicious canes on both hands.

Somehow you felt that he was intending to destroy this revolutionary idea that was in the school, you felt there was a real reason why he did more than he did normally, he was more vicious with us on this occasion than he had been when he'd caned us before. And we were all put down a class so that we were not in a high enough class to go in for the examination, the scholarship. That didn't make any difference to me because I was no scholar, but to some of my friends I'm sure they would have passed through that scholarship and would have gone to the grammar school in Norwich. It completely changed and upset the whole way of life for some of them.

Tony Kildwick

•

His size strikes you. He is a big man, over six foot tall. Gregarious, warm and charming, he laughs a lot. The founder member of a bikers' club in the fifties, motorbikes remain a great passion for him. An interest in genealogy has led to him publishing several books, and found him work tracing the family histories of Americans. His own background was wealthy, his early years in the 1920s were spent on his family's estate in Yorkshire.

•

Our family motto was *Fortita et Fidelito* which means 'Bravely and Faithfully.' This was instilled in me as something serious, it wasn't just a piece of heraldry, it summed up the attitude. In order to conform to that family tradition, there were certain things that one had to do – never to show emotion, that it was very unmanly to cry and to weep and the Englishman always sits here and only just makes very small gestures (only Frenchmen talk with their arms). 'Stop using your hands, dear,' they'd say to me. 'Just be quiet. Don't put yourself forward. Don't wear loud clothes.'

You didn't come down to breakfast every morning and say 'Don't forget the motto dear.' It was just taken for granted, it was just part of the training that one received. If I was getting very over-excited about anything like going to a party or getting a present, my mother would say, 'Stop jumping up and down, control yourself dear.'

This was the age of chivalry. I mean the great hero was King Arthur and the Knights of the Round Table and all that business. Looking after damsels in distress. I was always brought up to walk on the outside of the pavement when I was walking with a woman, to open the door for her, to get up when she came into the room, to be pleasant and charming to her. This was part of the training that one got. One's whole education was to make you a gentleman.

A gentleman I think was somebody who was brought up with the expectation that he would be holding some position of responsibility. In my case, the family firm I would be expected presumably to run in the time to come.

As children we were really, on the whole, much more fond of our nanny than of our parents. She got us up in the morning, she had a bedroom next to ours. We played and had tea in our day nursery and we slept in the night nursery. My mother sometimes brought us down for lunch but only when we were much older and were able to hold our knives and forks properly and not make a filthy mess. Up to about the age of six we were dressed up after tea, mother would come back from whatever she'd been doing, shopping, and we'd have to spend this hour or two with our parents. But really they were to some extent strangers.

They were scared witless by the fact that I might be contaminated by a Yorkshire or North Country accent. So I was sent, at the age of about eight, to boarding-school in the South, in order to get rid of my Yorkshire accent.

My mother was very anxious to do the right thing by me and of course the list of clothes one had to have at a prep school was enormous, two of everything, Eton collars and, you know, suits. We had a school cap which unfortunately couldn't be bought except at the school itself. So my mother wrote to the headmaster to find out what headgear should I wear to arrive at school. God knows what got into him because he said I could wear a bowler hat. I turned up at Waterloo Station with my grandparents and everybody, being frightfully butch about the whole thing wearing knickerbockers, plus-fours and a bowler hat. Well, all the other boys were wearing ordinary cloth caps. I was pitchforked into this train with all these other kids and sort of waved goodbye with my enormous suitcase. As soon as I got into the carriage, 'What you wearing that silly hat for?' I got bullied for that. I remember I just sat down and cried.

The excitement of getting there, and the misery of being separated from my parents was very great. There was one boy who had been told to look after me and the first thing he did was to run a mile rather than look after me. We were little beasts to one another.

I do remember very much crying of homesickness but I did it under the bedclothes so that the other boys wouldn't discover. I think they were all probably crying under the bedclothes if the truth

Tony Kildwick and a school friend taken in the early 1930s during their summer holidays.

were told, but one simply did not and should not show emotion even at that age. You had to keep your upper lip extremely stiff. It was absolutely ghastly.

Sport was so important because you had to be thought macho and butch. Football and cricket were compulsory because they are team games. You had to obey the rules and your team was part of something you owed allegiance to. I was hopeless at this sort of thing, partly because of my eyesight, I couldn't see, I couldn't play without my glasses. And if a ball came anywhere near me it either hit me on the head or I'd drop it or something like that. They thought I was wimpish and wet so I let the side down. I wasn't really doing what was expected of me. I was very good at music, I had a good singing voice and I played the piano. They thought this was unhealthy and this was the cause of a certain amount of bullying. I was just generally unpopular.

Bullying took the form of hiding your property. You see, in a prep school everything's done by bells, rather like prison. Get up, go to bed, go to meals, so forth and so on. You had to be bloody punctual and the way to be bullied was to hide something vital, a schoolbook for the next class or your shoes, football boots. The staff ought bloody well to have seen what was going on.

Everybody took it for granted. Nearly all the young masters had been killed in the war so the average age of the staff was very much older. They were all Victorians, they had all been brought up in a sort of Dickensian school.

I had a number of friends at my prep school who were equally sort of attacked. One of my closest friends was the son of a baronet, rather dreamy sort of character and we didn't conform to the idea of the chivalrous knight out on his horse to fight the foe.

I think my parents were pretty conscious of my not being very happy. I was very musical and the only prizes I ever won were for playing piano. I remember on one of my reports it strongly advised my parents to take me to a doctor because I spent far too much time playing the organ and far too little time playing ball.

I was extremely greedy as a youngster. Mars bars cost tuppence and we weren't allowed to eat them because they were sticky and sweet and bad for your stomach. Well, one day I was bet by one of my fellow pupils that I wouldn't break bounds and buy a couple of Mars bars. It was strictly forbidden to go outside the school grounds to the shops because you might catch some terrible disease you see. Anyhow I took him on and I went and as I came back I was caught by one of the masters. I got summoned in front of the whole school and I got twelve of the best. Up to that time I think I was always regarded as something of a wimp but because I kept my upper lip stiff and didn't blub I was the hero of the school for the rest of the term.

Frank Davies

•

There is a welcoming family atmosphere in Frank's comfortable semi-detached home in Salford. He is a serious, down-to-earth man with a very dry sense of humour. He has not moved from the area where he was born in 1921. His father was an engineer, and his mother was a full-time housewife. Both his parents had lost their previous partners, so Frank had five older step-brothers and sisters.

•

M e father was what you could call an old Cross Lane bruiser, he liked his pint, he liked his gambling and he lived a tough life, very rough. Me mother was just the opposite, you know, she came off a family where they were all a bit intellectual and went in for the higher things in life. This was when the trouble started, you know, there was family rows. There was always this difference of cultures between 'em.

Me father gave me mother just how much he thought she should have to bring the children up, the rest was his. He said, 'I work hard, it's my money.' Most of his was spent on the good life as far as he was concerned. He didn't even remember our birthdays. Many a time, you've had cards from yer mother and yer aunties and all the rest of it, all laid out on the mantelpiece, your father's come in and said, 'What's this for?'

'Oh it's your son's birthday.'

So he'd dip in his pocket and give you a couple of bob and that was the limit.

His idea was that men shouldn't cry and the odd occasions when I was growing up and I'd perhaps fall outside, or somebody's bashed you one, and you'd come in sobbing he really used to go to town on you. Shake you and say you weren't supposed to cry. 'You'll get more than that in life before long so get out there and hit 'em back.' He'd have you in the back yard, set of boxing gloves, showing you how to defend yourself. I can remember him kneeling down and I must have been just about level with him when he knelt down, so I was only a toddler, and he was teaching me then, some of the preliminaries of boxing. If there was any rumpus amongst ourselves, when you been larking with yer brothers: 'Right,' he'd say, 'in the yard with thee gloves on.' And that was it. Well, me being the youngest I used to get most of the pastings.

Me mother, on the other hand, used to try and lift us out of the gutter as it were. Me mother use to try and make us all learn things to sort of improve your education. She used to buy these books in parts weekly: Dickens, H.G. Wells, and encyclopaedias. Many a time we'd all have our heads stuck in a book by gas- or candlelight. Me father'd be ready to go out to the pub and he'd say, 'You're not going to sit in 'ere all night glued to those things are you?' His idea was that we should be out playing up the entries in the fresh air or roughing it a bit. 'You're going to end up an old woman,' he used to say. So me mother used to have to hide them in the end. She kept them under cover and, 'Shhh, he's gone. Right get the books out now.' And she'd be teaching us how to play chess. Then she'd say, 'Look at the time, he'll be home in a bit, put everything away.' And that would be it.

She was very big on music as well and she used to pay so much a week for me sisters to go to learn piano lessons. And when it came to my turn, when I got old enough, she decided to send me to learn the violin of all things.

Frank Davies aged seven (bottom row, second from left)
with his class at St Bartholomew's School,
Salford, in 1928.

•

She bought the violin, she used to get things on the weekly and booked me in with some violin teacher round the neighbourhood, you know, and it was about a shilling a week.

The first time me father saw it he couldn't believe it. He says, 'What's that for? You're not putting him on a bloody violin.' His idea like, was that he had a son that was going a bit weird, going playing a violin. It was unheard of to his way of thinking. It was anything but manly.

And you can imagine, the first time I walked out with this violin case and all yer old mates waiting. The crowd I was associated with were all a rum crowd. Always looking for some adventure and as soon as they see you walking down the street with a violin case that was it. 'Where you going with that?' They were all following you. 'You're not going for violin playing are you?' That was looked upon as effeminate, you were a Mary-Anne to play a violin so I had to run the gauntlet.

That was my limit. I could read and do indoors but after me mates had been calling me names, sissy and that, a few times I just refused to go to the violin lessons. Me and my mother were arguing about it, she's telling me to go and I was saying I wouldn't and she hit me with the damn thing, broke it over my head. So that was the end of the violin.

Danny Slattery

•

Since retiring from his job as a security guard, Danny has finished renovating and decorating his turn-of-the-century terraced house. He is now enjoying life with his wife in South London, where he was born and raised. He is a reformed alcoholic, saved by Alcoholics Anonymous who he now campaigns for. He often sits out in his back garden, looks back on the past and thinks 'I'm a lucky man'. Danny was evacuated with his school from the Elephant and Castle in 1940, when he was ten years old. All the children from the school were sent to Gillingham in Dorset, where Danny was billeted with a wealthy elderly couple living in a country cottage.

•

I enjoyed being evacuated. I enjoyed being away from London, away from my mum I suppose. It was something new that I'd never seen before. It was just another change in my life that was happening to me. And we'd never seen cows, sheep or anything like, before, not in real life anyway and we used to run round the fields, rounding 'em up, making out we were cowboys. 'Course, then we used to get into trouble, get told off and brought to the headmaster. I got into two or three scrapes.

One day we was wandering across the fields and we came to some allotments, we got into one of the sheds. Why I done that I don't know but it was just an adventure. We broke in and we got all the tools out and threw them in the local canal.

The lady I was evacuated with was a bit of a church woman, you know, and she'd given me this big red schoolboy's cap and I was the only one in the village that used to wear that hat and I was identified easily. Someone had seen me running away from the

Evacuee children at Eastbourne in September 1939. Over a million school children were evacuated that year causing mass disruption to family life and contributing to the big increase in crime amongst boys during the Second World War.

•

sheds. I can remember a big sergeant come and questioned me about it and I owned up straightaway.

Then I got involved with the Court. It was kind of a big hall with three old gentlemen sitting there and I think I was fined five shillings. The court had a whip round and paid it. But after that the old lady'd had enough of me and they said I had to go back to London and my mother had to come and get me and take me home even though the bombing was on.

I never had a father, my father died when I was four years old, so I had a bit of a run, a bit of a free 'and. Me mother used to go out early morning cleaning and I had to get meself up. She used to leave a note on the table, 'don't forget to eat your sop', then I had to get meself off to school. But not all the kids were back 'cos some of them was still evacuated and so there was times when I didn't go to school, you know, I used to go round to my mates.

We had a little gang, about five or six of us, and we all used to run around together playing on a bombed ruin which was our play-ground. We used to call it going to war, let's have a war with so and so street. One 'ud throw a stone and then all of a sudden we'd get barri-cades, throwing bricks. A couple of times somebody would get really injured like, you know, a brick on the head or you'd be running away and you'd get a brick in the middle of the back, but that was all part and parcel of growing up like. If you really showed courage and sort of advanced with a brick in yer hand, and they all run away like, you was the lad then.

Then many times we used to break into shops, 'cos most of them then were blasted with the bombs, no problem breaking into it 'cos probably the door was hanging off anyway. I can remember we broke into one place and got a lot of egg powder. I remember it used to have stars and stripes on it, it was really nice, everybody liked it so we nicked a big box of that.

I can remember one day we were all standing there, talking and skylarking about, and three plain clothes coppers – they were called Splits in them days, you could tell 'em a mile away, 'cos they all wore these white macs – they got 'old of us, like grabbed 'old of us all and pushed us against the shutters and asked for identity cards. Of course my mother wouldn't let me have mine 'cos I was so irresponsible and they took us down to Carter Street. You got a smack round the earhole or sometimes a punch in the face off the

Danny Slattery (left) on a day trip with his family in 1936. After the death of his father in 1934, Danny started getting into trouble both at home and in school.

•

law, and you just accepted it. Then our mothers had to come and bail us out.

I was car mad at that time. The leather seats, the smell of petrol, it used to do something to me. It was an impulse to want to drive so we used to steal cars sometimes, just drive off. They was easy to get into and we got quite experienced going round the back turnings to try and keep out of the way of anyone we knew. I think the adrenalin used to get going. You'd say, 'The Police!' And whoever was driving just used to slam his foot down. We had no idea of changing gear or anything like that. You just went and stopped in a turning and everybody scattered.

We used to go to English Martyr School in Rodney Road and most of it was like religion, about God and Mary and Jesus. We had to go to church every Sunday and they used to tell us about our soul and I used to picture in my mind's eye that my soul was like white, it was really white, and directly I sinned a black mark would come on it and if I sinned again another black mark, you know, and the way I was getting into trouble and doing things, well as far as I was concerned my soul was completely black, inside me. Then when we went to confession we had to tell all. I was terrified of God, or Jesus. So when it was my turn I would go in and just tell him everything, that you swore, that I was disobedient to me mother, that I'd stolen stuff, all sorts of things. I used to really sort things out and once I'd done all me confessing about meself I really and truly believed that my soul was white again, pure white. So when I walked out of that church I felt as if I was clean and pure.

David Swift

•

David lives in Nottingham in a huge old farmhouse which he and his wife Irene have lovingly restored. The restorations have taken both years of work and ingenuity. David is a cartoonist with a great sense of humour. Born in 1930 into a harsh mining family, it was soon discovered that David had a type of muscular dystrophy. Although his condition worsened as he grew older, he struggled to hide his disability and to fit in with the rough and tumble street life of his working-class childhood.

•

I didn't want to be considered a freak. We have in Nottingham a Goose Fair and in them days they used to have all the side shows and have all the freaks in the side shows and I used to go in and somebody once said to me, 'You ought to be in a side show, you could be a freak.' That really got to me, you know, and I wanted to prove that I wasn't a freak. I wanted to say, 'Well, look I'm all right, don't bother me.'

If you told people, 'Well, I've got a disease', nobody would come near you, but if you told them that it was as a result of falling down a conker tree, then it was something that you got in battle, you know, it was just stories to hide the situation.

In their games there was only so much I could do. I could be a cowboy that had been injured, that had fallen off a horse in a rodeo. Or I could be somebody that had been shot or run over by something. Because I'd been shot in the leg you see that was acceptable, to be injured, to come home with a war wound was very acceptable. In some way then you were considered manly.

I could always sit and play cards or pitch and toss. Then when I got to fourteen I couldn't pick anything off the floor, 'cos my thumbs wouldn't pick up. And when my brothers noticed my hands they says, 'He deals them fucking cards like sandwiches.' And then you'd be so humiliated because you knew you were different, but what could you do?

I didn't want to stand out in any way. They wanted to give me the sportsman of the year cup at school so I said, 'Why do you want to give it to me?' 'Cos I hadn't done anything special.

So the master says, 'It's because you're disabled and you've been managing to play football.'

I said, 'Well I don't want it. I don't want to be sportsman of the year on that ground, I want to be sportsman of the year 'cos I'm good at sport, not because I'm disabled.'

I wanted to be included, I didn't want to be left out when they started to play these games. I mean when they started to pick a football team I was always picked last but I didn't mind as long as I were picked.

Sport was so important to me, but I'd get all that name calling again on the sidelines with people watching. 'They must be bad if they've got a fucking cripple playing for 'em.'

And the cross-country racing. You either went on the cross-country race or you stopped at school and did 500 lines – 'Why I have not joined the cross-country race'. I'd have sooner gone on the cross-country race than do all those lines and feel humiliated again because I'd got to explain why. I always remember being on this race, it was so painful for me. It was about three miles and three miles was a long way and I had to keep stopping and starting. I was trying to take short-cuts, but there weren't any, and it was misty and foggy. By the end everybody had left me and I was on my own in the mist, you know, trying to find my way back to school, trying to run or walk. I remember going through the school playground, through the gates and the headmaster meeting me. I were red-faced and out of breath and sick and ill and me legs was throbbing, everything was.

He said, 'You're very late Swift, you're too late for your dinner.' He wanted to announce it in assembly that even though I was disabled I had finished the race. And I hated him for that because I didn't want everybody to know that I were last out of three hundred and odd pupils.

I used to go off into this wooded area, quite a few acres of it, and I used to long to go in there on my own. I used to take my shoes off and my clothes off and run through the woods and I used to lay there in the trees with nothing on. I used to go swimming in the canal but I always seemed to be alone. I couldn't seem to get another pal, a personal pal, because I couldn't do the things that they could do.

CHAPTER TWO

Rites Of Manhood

───────────── • ─────────────

In 1944 fourteen-year-old Ron McGill began work as a telegraph boy, delivering telegrams from the post office in Hammersmith, West London. 'As soon as you arrived you were fitted out with your new uniform. I thought, this is nice, I feel good. Then they told me I was going to be bogged. The senior telegraph boys grabbed me, turned me upside-down, held me over the toilet, lowered my head and pulled the chain. I struggled and they banged my head on the side of the pan. Out I came and they told me I had been initiated. That was called bogging.'

Workplace and apprenticeship initiations like this used to be a fact of life in most industries and were remembered by many of the men we interviewed, often with laughter. Boys were expected to take it all

The 'banging out' of an apprentice at the Glovers factory in Chelsea, 1950. Initiation ceremonies like this marked the acceptance of young workers into the adult world.

•

Above: 'Clocking in' at a
factory in the 1930s. Taking
home the first pay packet was
an important rite of passage,
after which the new worker
began to be treated as a young
adult by his family.

Smoking, portrayed in films of the time as glamorous and
sophisticated, was a badge of masculinity for young men.

in good part and after their initiation they usually joined the tormentors of the next set of new recruits. But for more sensitive boys like Harold Smith who began work in an engineering factory in Manchester during the last war it was a nightmare. 'They'd get your trousers down and rub axle grease all over you. It was rape really and I didn't want to be initiated.'

There was often a strong sexual element in the ritual humiliation of the new boy. The victim's trousers would be pulled down and his genitals smeared with oil, tar or grease. It was a kind of public statement that the 'virgin' boy had arrived in the adult world and would have to face up to its harsh realities. He was now 'one of us', like it or not. It was a rite of passage helping to mark the transition from boyhood to manhood.

If there was one defining moment when our interviewees felt they grew up and began to be treated like adults, it was when they started a full-time job. For most working-class boys between the wars this coincided with their fourteenth birthday: they left school on the Friday and began work the following Monday. The weekly pay packet, usually handed over unopened to Mum, gave the young worker a new status and importance in the family. In exchange for the money – which could significantly raise the standard of living in working-class homes – the boy was given new privileges. Many recall being bought their first pair of long trousers and enjoying more food on their plate, relief from domestic chores and permission to stay out later at night. They were also given pocket money which could be spent on displays of masculinity.

In a culture that placed great emphasis on manliness, boys in their teens were keen to prove to themselves and others that they were 'men'. They emulated what the men did: smoking, drinking and sporting a few fashion items like the trilby hat popularized by American film stars. To begin with much was done secretly for fear of parental disapproval, but by the time they reached their late teens most felt comfortable going into a pub – in those days still very much male territory – to smoke and drink with their fathers. Frank Davies and Joe Crofts, both teenagers in the North of England between the wars, remember in amusing detail their attempts (sometimes bungled and ridiculous) to establish their new manly image. Wilf Page, who left his village home in Norfolk in 1927 to enter domestic service, felt the job he was doing was unmanly. He finally

resolved this when he joined the RAF.

Working-class boys generally grew up more quickly than their middle-class counterparts. Some of the men we interviewed who enjoyed an extended education at grammar school, public school, college and university, felt that being protected from the adult world made them less sure of themselves as young men.

During the early years of the century there was a growing recognition that puberty or adolescence was a universal stage of life, supposedly characterized by insecurity, self-doubt and emotional turbulence. These new psychological theories probably applied most of all to middle-class youth amongst whom these feelings seem to have been most pronounced. One of the landmarks for them in growing up was becoming a senior boy or prefect. Sidney Ling was a pupil at Ipswich Grammar School in the 1920s.

'One of the things I remember mostly in my advancement from boyhood to manhood was when I was made a prefect and I had a black book and if any boy spat or swore or laughed, their name went in my prefect book and they had to do detention. When I was made a prefect this had a psychological effect on me because it reminded

Above: *Morning roll call at Harrow School in the 1930s. Public schools were based on a strictly disciplined regime, training boys to become leaders of men.*

Left: *Young miners in the 1940s waiting for the cage to take them down the pit for their shift. It was important for their macho image that they did not show any fear.*

•

Weight-lifting at Acton Sports Club in 1946. Body-building classes like this were
enormously popular amongst young men keen to develop a masculine physique –
the League of Health and Strength had a membership of over
125 000 men at this time.

•

me that the headmaster had got faith in me, which was quite something and it built my ego.'

Another landmark was to play for the school team. But for boys
like Alec Gunn, a pupil at Sherborne public school in the 1930s, who
neither wanted to administer beatings (a prime duty of a prefect at
the school) nor to play rugby or cricket for his house team, feelings
of personal inadequacy invariably followed.

Body changes and physical development have of course always
underpinned the personality change from boy into man. These perhaps took on new significance in a culture where masculinity was so
highly regarded. Shaving – in particular the use of a cut-throat razor
– was a very important emblem of manhood in the first decades of
the century.

Dave Bowman remembers in the 1930s, 'Without doubt, shaving with an open razor was very macho, particularly if you were
at camp with the Scouts or the Boys' Brigade. And then came

shaving time in the morning and you soaped your face and you got your hands up with this big open razor and "ooh, he's good, he's a man he is, ooh he's very good, very macho". But there's a fellow with his little safety razor digging in here and there, "ooh not macho at all".

Bodily strength had to be demonstrated in ritual display. This meant fighting and not showing fear – an important badge of manliness. The status of a young man (especially in poorer working-class areas) was governed to a large extent by his ability to fight. In the street, the playing fields and the workplace, young men fought to establish their position in the pecking order. Very often it would be a fist fight – observing the Queensberry Rules – watched by friends or workmates. One barometer of the increasing interest in body development and strength was the growth of exercise and body-building clubs like the League of Health and Strength, which by the late 1930s boasted a membership of around 125 000 young men in over 400 'physical culture' clubs.

George Ryder began work on a building site in Liverpool in 1936 as a slightly built fourteen-year-old. He quickly turned to body-building as a way of holding his own amongst the older boys:

George Ryder was a keen body builder. He is photographed here on holiday in the 1930s.

When I went in as an apprentice bricklayer I didn't smoke, I didn't drink, and it was foreign to me to find people who drank and smoke the way they did in the building trade. Because of this they used to think 'this fellow's a sissy' and I got many a thump. So in the end I had to really stand up for myself. Three or four nights a week I used to do weight-lifting, body-building, until you managed to get a reasonably good body. And of course when you took your shirt off and you had a bit of muscle, they'd look at you a little bit askance and think, well, I'm staying away from him. So really the pecking order sorted itself out. That was the way you became a man really because you had to show yourself that you were strong, you had to prove yourself that you were as good as they were.

•

Tattoos were also important badges of masculinity for young men in the first decades of the century, particularly in the armed forces. Tom Parton served with the British Army in India in the 1920s. 'I'd been in India five years before I got the tattoos on. Practically half the regiment had tattoos and they was beginning to think that I was a softie because I hadn't got any. Although I used to play rugby they thought I was soft and that's one of the reasons I got these on, made me look tough.'

One of the most important arenas of all for proving manhood was of course sexual experience. But before the 1950s sex before marriage was taboo and most institutions involved in moulding the minds of young people tried to postpone any early interest in the opposite sex. Many of our interviewees – especially those, like Alec Gunn, who went to boarding-schools – remember dire warnings of the dangers of masturbation. Schools, churches and youth clubs made strenuous efforts to keep the sexes apart and encouraged the idea that it was manly to exercise self-control. But sexual desire would not go away. The forbidden nature of sex made it all the more enticing and exciting for young men eager to prove themselves. As many were ignorant about sex and fearful of its consequences, prostitutes played an important role in the sexual initiation of many young men. Geordie Todd remembers how losing your virginity in this way could be a very public – and rather disappointing – rite of passage.

The few sex surveys that were done prior to the 1950s suggest that the number of people having sex before marriage was gradually increasing from the 1900s onwards. But memories of illicit sex in fields, back alleys and parents' living-rooms, reveal how little pleasure was involved. Most important for the young men, it seems, was notching up a sexual conquest to impress friends and confirm their manly status. The reverse was true for a young woman who, if she agreed to sex too easily, won the reputation of being 'easy' and 'bad', which could wreck her marriage chances.

Albert Gomes's memory of his first sexual experience in Liverpool in the 1930s vividly sums up the attitudes of the day:

In those days girls who were morally loose or easy pickings were consid-ered scrubbers. The girl I first had sex with was somebody from another district entirely and I met her on a bike ride. I'd just turned fourteen

Top: *Sexual experience was the ultimate rite of passage to manhood.*

Above: *George Ryder and his girlfriend photographed in the 1930s. George grew up in Kirkdale, Liverpool, were he worked as a brick layer until he joined the army in 1940.*

•

Two lads getting the brush-off in the early fifties.
Groups of young men and women would parade up and down the 'Monkey Run'
on Saturday nights hoping to make a date with a partner.

•

and it was during the summer holidays. And we went round the back of
this cemetery and she apparently decided to acquiesce, but in her own
way, so she pretended not to be aware of what was going on, to be asleep
in other words. I was over-excited and it wasn't a very satisfactory per-
formance I'm afraid. And she rode her bicycle home. I told two of my
closest pals that I'd cracked it, and I don't know if they'd cracked it but
if they hadn't they made sure that they showed soon afterwards that
they'd caught up with me because we all wanted to be at the same level.

•

Full sexual experience was for many the last rite of passage into manhood. Although boys had to grow up quickly by coping in the adult
world of work, sexual relationships often began much later, in the
late teens and early twenties, and many waited until they were married. Some recall that it was only when they were married that they
finally felt accepted by their family and friends as fully-grown adults.
George Ryder who married at the age of 23 in 1945 remembers:
'when I got married it seemed to break down a barrier with my

father. He started to talk to me like a friend, sort of like an equal at last. It was only when you had your own family and your own chattels around you that were seen as a real man.'

Wilf Page

•

When he was fifteen Wilf left his village home in Norfolk to start work as a servant in a large house in Baldock, Hertfordshire. Due to unemployment in Norfolk he was forced to turn his back on the traditional rural life of an agricultural labourer, and did not want to work with his scrap merchant father. He remembers the shock and excitement as a young man, of waving goodbye to his mother, father and three sisters and beginning an independent life.

•

Our headmaster used to say to us, 'Now then, you're going out to earn a living, to work hard and play hard. Remember what you've learned at school, save a bit of money and you'll have an exciting time.' But as soon as we left school and got out into the world we found there was eleven million other people looking for this work.

There was nothing at home for me so I had to take a job in service a long way off in Hertfordshire, a big place called Weston Park. I had to up sticks and take my few belongings to live in and work as a servant. There was nothing else for it but to leave home.

I went on the bus and when I got off at the place where someone from the hall was going to meet me I'll never forget I heard somebody shouting, 'Is Mr Page here?' And I thought, 'Who the hell's Mr Page? And suddenly it struck, 'Oh, it must be me.'

For the first time I thought, 'God, here I am out in the big world, I'm no longer Wilf, the boy Wilf. Here I am, a man, Mr Wilfred Page. Fancy, here I am miles away from home, suddenly all on my own, got to protect myself and see after myself without any protection from the family at all.' It was a shattering experience to have that happen to you, you know, to suddenly find that you are suddenly a man, a grown-up man. And as I went, as the chauffeur took me to the house in the car I was very quiet and he kept saying, 'What's the matter with you, are you nervous or something?' I said, 'No, not really, I'm

Wilf Page at the age of fifteen in 1928. His first job was a servant at Weston Park in Hertfordshire.

•

looking at the beautiful scenery.' But I wasn't really, I was thinking to myself, 'God, I'm mister Page, I'm Mr Page, where do I go to from here, who do I go to if I've got a problem, what do I do about it?'

First I went in the kitchen and I worked there for about a week, I suppose, and this damned iron boiler thing, I couldn't get it to light in the mornings. I used to light it and it used to blaze up and suddenly it would die down again. I couldn't master this at all. Then they put me into the pantry to work with the butler and I worked there for several months but I felt it wasn't a man's job. I'd been brought up to believe that men were men and somehow waiting at table with white gloves on wasn't a man's job. So I decided to go back home.

But however glad I was to be home there was still no work when I got there and so with a friend of mine I hitch-hiked to London. We got a lift from a bloke with some dead pigs he was taking to Smithfield market and I had to sleep in the back with these pigs, terrible.

We didn't know anything about London and it was very frightening to us because we were both kids who had come from a village atmosphere and to be in London in this condition was terrible. Fortunately I'd got a year's work behind me with that house, so I did have a card and I could get twelve and six a week dole that kept us going. We had to just buy cheap food. But we couldn't get anywhere to stay so we were sleeping rough in Green Park. The *News of the*

World was a very big paper and it used to cover you up very well in those days. We used to wrap ourselves in that on the seats. But being out at night in London was terrible because it was quite unnatural, lonely. And the longer you stayed there the more dishevelled you got. We used to go into the men's toilets at Charing Cross to try and look a bit respectable, get a bit of a wash.

We both felt somehow we shouldn't have left home and then we felt, 'Well, if we do go back we're a failure, we've got to stay here now.' We'd sort of burned our boats and told all our mates that we were going up to London to earn some money.

The terrible thing was that when you went for a job you'd find there'd be about forty people in front of you. I was fortunate, in that I was a very young lad, pink-cheeked, country lad, and looked as if I was the kind of image they wanted behind a bar as against some of the poor devils in front of me, who'd been hunting for work for years, so I got a job eventually working in a pub in Kensington.

But as soon as I started, it was living in and I found out what it was like. The other lads there were going out in the evenings after closing time and having a booze up, taking bottles of beer out with them, and whisky. They'd got two or three women and all kinds of sexual behaviour took place and there was me, still got a lot of the old Methodist Sunday School thought in my mind. I thought, 'God Wilf, you're going to be an old reprobate if you carry on like this, you got to do something about it.'

Wilf Page joined the RAF in 1933 and went on to train as an aerial photographer.

•

I thought I wanted some discipline. Anyway, just opposite the war memorial was a notice saying 'Vacancies for the RAF'. So I went to the address and I said, 'What are all the vacancies about?' And he said, 'Well, what we do, we recruit about 150 to 200 people in the RAF every January – they're people who are out of work or haven't got any jobs, haven't got any homes, people who are barrow boys, newspaper boys, anybody, then from January you're training, physical training, for the Royal Tournament in June and then you are in the display for the RAF as an advert, what can be done with people who are down-and-outs and hungry.'

I just had a medical to go and join there and then. And it turned out like he said. The RAF used to show us off as people who had been lazy loafers out in the street and what they'd done with us and what a wonderful team they'd built up. It was me there at the Royal Tournament marching with my uniform on. And oh it was a wonderful experience to do that, I thoroughly enjoyed it. I liked having the audience around me, you know, thousands of people watching you, you know, as you marched into this great arena. Masses of people cheering for me who a few months ago was serving beer in a pub and feeling very low and you were in the RAF defending the country.

I felt this sort of thing couldn't happen to me, I mean, I was just a nobody to suddenly get all this applause and shouting that was confined to films and film stars. It gave you a tremendous boost. I felt somehow that now I'd really got on my feet. I was a full-grown man with plenty of qualifications. I was now being trained and that really did make me feel at last I was growing up.

Geordie Todd

•

Geordie was born in 1912 in North Shields, the youngest of thirteen children. His father was a miner, and his mother divided her time between the vegetable shop she part-owned, and her work as a herring splitter. She also adopted three more children after Geordie and his four brothers and sisters were born. She died when Geordie was eleven and, within twelve months, his father remarried a much younger woman. They had five children together.

•

Me father got married the second time and when he brought her home I thought everything would just carry on as usual, which it did do for the first month or so. Then things started to deteriorate. She started to rule the roost, she wanted me out the house. Every time I came in from school she used to tell me father I'd taken such and such out of her purse and I used to get a thrashing and of course soon as I could I used to be out the house and away, on to the fish quay. That was me second home.

I was forever down there watching the fishermen and messing around and swimming with me pals. It was bravado, who could beat the other one. And in the winter months there was an ice store on the quay and it discharged into the fish quay and made what we called the 'hots'. We used to just dive off about what twelve, fourteen feet. All the girls on the quay used to be shouting down and you used to swim out, no swimsuit on and you just used to turn on your back and start to float and the girls used to say 'Ooh'. They'd be looking twice as hard like, it was great fun.

But things at home didn't get any better at all and the final time my stepmother accused me, she'd told me father on me again and he just reached up over the fireplace like where the strap was always hanging. I said, 'No way are you going to use that on me again, those days are finished. I just out the door and down the stairs and said I wasn't going back, which I never did.

'Course I went straight to the quay. I had nowhere else to turn. I was too young to go on the trawlers, I was only about fifteen, so I went with a chap called Charlie Wood in a coal boat. I was only a boy, I was on a half-share of the money and I was sleeping on the boat as well. But it was all work and I was feeling a little bit badly done to 'cos I could mend the nets and I could splice but I wasn't getting full money, so I left him.

I was looking round for a go on the trawlers. I tried two or three of the skippers and of course the first word they said, 'Have you been to sea before in the trawlers?' I says, 'Bloody hell, that's what I want to

Geordie Todd (left) *with the crew of the* Morning Star. *He was fourteen years old when he left school to become a fisherman.*

•

serve me time for.' In the end one of them took me on for like a trial. Fair enough, so away we went to sea. I had no sea boots or nothing, just a pair of half wellies, no oilskins. But I stuck it trip after trip and the skipper asked me did I think I'd like it. 'Oh yes, I like it all right,' I said. 'I'm all for it.' I got signed on as a deck boy, for one and six a day, and I did anything from twelve to eighteen hours a day. I was called out during the night too for hauling the gear, gut the fish, wash it and hand it down below. I cracked ice for the mate for to spread on the shelves for to put the fish on.

As the time went on the skipper increased me money then within a few short months I was the best-paid man aboard the boat, and I was the youngest one. I was well-off then and I was buying a suit, made to measure and all mind, and bowler hat, silk scarf. Oh I was a dandy then.

It was every young lad's dream to go out with the girls like. You used to posh yourself up. I was never really attached to one girl. Now and again you'd have a bit squeeze and then you'd get a slap across the lug and that put you off. We used to come out the pictures, walk along to where they lived and I'd say, 'Goodnight'. They used to often say, 'We'll see you next trip?' 'Lord knows, I don't. I might have met somebody else then.'

We'd all go to the pictures together and you may have one boy in the crowd a little bit older and he would be smoking his head off and he used to say, 'Here you are Geordie, have a puff.' And of course, macho, and you had a puff, sort of style. You used to just stand on the edge of the seat and get a light from the gas bracket. There might be three of you together and three or four girls and of course you wasn't even looking at the pictures. Old daft carry-on, cuddling each other and kissing each other.

You heard the chaps on the trawler talking, always talking about sex and girls. But I was eighteen before I had any sex and that was with a prostitute. I was friendly with another hand, he was about twenty-four, and one night we're still in our sea boots, working gear, then he says, 'Lad, I'll introduce you. Come with me.' Naturally I went with him and we walked up the stairs on to the town square into this house. Me following, just like a little dog. This older woman, I think she would be forty, was there. He spoke to her and next thing I knew his flies were undone and she was having a gander and he paid her summat and he says, 'Go on, let her have a look.' I was a bit flabbergasted like, so your flap drops down like that and she just put her hand in and took me privates out. She says, 'All right, that'll be three bob.' I says, 'Bloody hell, that's two days pay.'

She allocated a room to us like and I went in and the girl was there, in bed, starkers. She just said something like, 'Let's get on with it.' She helped us and next thing I knew it was God bless you and all over, done and finished. I was coming out the door and my mate was standing waiting on us. He asked me how did it go and I says, 'Well, I didn't expect that, but I'm bloody broke now.'

Of course mind, when we went to sea next day, and the first haul, and we're all in the pond gutting, the deckie he says, 'Oh I brought the lad away and he's been and had his nookies'. I said, 'What d'you want to tell 'em for?' In two minutes the whole boat knew about it and of course that's the main conversation when they're gutting, is girls and sex. I was one of the crew, I was fully grown up then. I knew I'd done something, I'd become a little, a sort of man, I'd sown some wild oats and that was it sort of style. I think it was a relief.

Alec Gunn

•

He wears a cravat and a smile and the room is decorated with flowers from the large garden which surrounds the Surrey home he shares with his wife, Bay. His received pronunciation and diction hint at the actor he dreamed of being as an unhappy boarding-school boy in the early 1930s. It was an ambition he fulfilled briefly after a commission in the Second World War, before fatherhood and family responsibility turned him reluctantly away from the theatre. He retired in 1980 from a career spent in commercial television – Alec was the first transmission controller at Rediffusion, and he took on the same role when LWT began. He now spends his free time writing – he has completed three volumes of his autobiography – and recording books for the blind.

•

I arrived at Sherbourne at the beginning of the summer term in 1932 with my mother. I met my housemaster and you know it's odd isn't it that he had this obsession about corporal punishment. He said to my mother, 'Of course he will have to be smacked'. And my

*Alec Gunn in 1934 (fourth from the right on the front row) during his time at
Sherbourne. Its regimentation came as a shock to Alec after the liberal atmosphere of his prep
school, The Dragon School in Oxford.*

mother, who was very against it, was quite upset by this and they had
a long talk together while I was left alone. My mother was trying to
persuade him that she didn't want her son smacked, but a fat lot of
good it did.

The whole ethos at Sherbourne was to toughen people up, brace
up, no slacking. Wonderful phrase that my housemaster used to use,
'No slacking on the footer field'. In his form he had a big sign which
said, 'Learn to bite the granite, not suck the jujubes of life.' That sums
up Sherbourne completely.

There was a complete glorification of games and there wasn't
much encouragement to be good at work. If you were a good classi-
cal scholar that was all right, but History and English were considered fairly suspect. They had visions of poets in long hair and floppy
ties and atheists like Shelley. Shakespeare was all right because there
were lots of wars in it. And classics were meant to be the sort of thing
that toughened up the brain in the way that games toughened up the
body. The whole basis of Latin and Greek was considered manly.

They were very good at games and played rugby and cricket.
There were tennis courts but you never had any tuition – not being a
team game it was considered effeminate. Rugger and cricket were

men's games, tennis was a game for girls.

Slacking on the footer field was considered one of the biggest crimes of all and you'd undoubtedly get beaten for it by a prefect. Rugger was considered a good game, a toughening up game. If it meant smashed collar bones they were worn almost as a badge of honour. Boys would go about with this enormous bandage on and it was considered a damm good show really.

Luckily for me rugby was the one game I think where you can put on a performance, where you can puff and blow and appear to be pushing and appear to be frightfully keen and not do a great deal. Especially if you're a forward. My acting talents came into force quite early, really. I mean you can look exhausted rather like Donald Wolfitt hanging on the curtain at the end of a curtain call, it's not difficult.

You had your all-powerful housemaster and he had his prefects who ran a very, very tight ship indeed. We had ginger weeks when the housemaster would decide we were getting slack. That meant you doubled everywhere, you had to parade outside after a cold shower in the morning, you had to parade outside in the yard fully dressed. We wore stiff collars so if you lost a stud there was an absolute panic. You then had to be inspected by a prefect and if a boy was not tidy and not clean and hair not brushed he got beaten. You were twice as likely to get beaten in a ginger week as you were any other time.

They had a system of crosses in the changing room. If you left your shorts on the floor or something you got one cross. Two crosses then you got two strokes, three crosses it went up accordingly. So if a prefect disliked you he just got a pair of shorts from your locker and left 'em on the floor and then they could cane you.

After prep in the evening was execution time so if you were discovered by a prefect to have committed some crime early in the day, you were told you'd be beaten that night. So in other words you had all day to think about it, which I think was particularly unpleasant. If you were giggling in prep or something then you were beaten after prep. At the time of executions you were taken into the large bathroom. The rest of the house could hear all the swishing going on.

The boys would run to the study where the bell had rung and the prefect would say, 'Send Gunn to me'. So you trotted along and he said something like, 'There was a bit of milk on this jug. Come with me.' He went into this place with all the washbasins, you bent over it, pulled your coat up and were caned. It was extremely painful and unpleasant.

But one was afraid to be afraid, one was afraid to show fear. I think one would have been petrified of crying. Yes, one always had tears in one's eyes but you suppressed them, you'd be considered such a wimp. I'd feel sore when it had happened, humiliated. The whole thing was so very unnecessary. That isn't keeping discipline, that's just damn silly.

There was always a parade to see the scars, that was the great thing. After you were beaten everybody wanted to have a look at the stripes. They were sort of badges of honour, particularly if you'd had six. All rather nasty actually. Some boys undoubtedly did get pleasure out of all this but I think others were just part of the system and didn't really hit you very hard. It was just a thing that was expected of one, it was almost impossible not to do. Of course when I was made a prefect to my shame I beat a boy myself once, only once. It was a boy called Morgan and I only gave him taps and he was embarrassed and I was embarrassed. I never beat a boy again. It was just that I hadn't got the guts to go against the system and somebody said, 'You must beat him, he's done this on your patch.' I've forgotten what the crime was completely. I was a prefect by then and I hadn't got the courage to opt out.

I had a crush on another boy, I think we all did that. I must have made it fairly obvious because I asked to share a study with him. There was nothing physical about it, but I was fairly keen on him. I went to the Housemaster and said could I share a study with this boy and the wily old thing twigged, you see, because he was a very attractive-looking boy and he said, 'No', and read me a long lecture. He just said, 'Romantic friendships are the very devil and I can't encourage them.'

Sex education at Sherbourne was a little bit inadequate. One's Housemaster asked one in about the age of puberty for half an hour's chat. The chat consisted of the facts of life which weren't all that accurate. He was after all a bachelor who certainly had no experience of that sort of thing whatsoever. The main theme of the Soul Saver was masturbation. He said that it was a very bad thing to do and if I were tempted I should say to myself, 'My name is Alexander Gunn and I will not be a slave to it.'

Joe Crofts

•

He is an easy-going, handsome seventy-two-year old with a broad Yorkshire accent. He lives with his wife, Marie, in a large semi-detached house on the outskirts of Preston. They have four children, the last two were surprise twins, born when Joe and Marie were both in their late forties. Now the children have left home, Joe spends a lot of time cycling around the countryside, covering distances that would tire a much younger man. Joe was born in the mining village of Beighton, near Sheffield. His father was a collier so it was taken for granted that Joe would join him in the pit as soon as he left school. He remembers, with a wry shake of his head, his first day at work.

•

M e father had no choice because he could have lost his job by not bringing me into the pit or at least he could have got in

The scene underground in a Derbyshire pit in 1910.
The boy on the right is only thirteen years old.
Working class boys went to work
as soon as possible to help boost the family income.

•

the bad books of the management. When I were coming up to going down pit, manager said to my father, 'I see you've got a lad coming up for working age Joe, I want to see him up in my office'. That meant he had to see you up in his office. So I left school on Friday and I started in pit at Monday. I were fourteen. The week before you couldn't sleep thinking about it. It was something you knew you were always going to do but when the day came you were a little bit apprehensive you know.

I can remember walking down road, it was a three-mile walk, with me father. We had tin bottles, we called them Dudley's, full of water, three pints of water and me father had found me one of his old caps out and some chewing-gum which later turned to chewing tobacco.

And going for first time down cage. A cage drops fast. Your ears pop when you go down and it goes black dark straightaway. I wasn't frightened, I was more dismayed. I'd always been a lad as was a nature lover. I spent most of my free time around woods, animal-watching, and on afternoon shifts to suddenly plunge, see a beautiful summer afternoon plunge down into darkness while ten and half-past ten at night and you'd missed all that lovely summer afternoon …

At pit bottom there was the dank smell of spent air. You just got a two-volt lamp and it used to burn 'oles in all yer pants, acid juice run out of 'em and sometimes they'd conk out even before shift were up. Me father says, 'Look, I'll leave you in charge of this chap like.' That were Deputy and I remember the feeling of aloneness you know. Anyhow Deputy took me to place of work. I were doing me shift with some more lads, lads my age. You were haulage lads and it were your job to get the tubs to the men on the coal face.

I remember thinking at the end of the shift, 'I'm not going to be black to go 'ome'. I picked dust up and rubbed it on me face to make sure I were black, like a miner should be when he went 'ome. When you come 'ome first day you're really proud. You're black and other kids are just coming home from school and I said, 'I'm not getting washed yet mum, I want to leave me muck on a bit like.' I can see me mother now putting her arms round me, like she hugged me to and that's one of the few times I can remember her like really hugging. And they were laughing because they all realized that I'd rubbed me face with muck to look dirtier. There were hand marks down me face. And you strutted a bit in front of school mates, then went and

Joe Crofts aged sixteen. By this time he had been working down the pit for two years.

•

had a bath. Then it was in front of fire having a bath in tin tub. While me father had a bath me and me mother went out and while I had a bath they went out and that's how it were, aye.

On this particular run where we took the tubs to the coal face there was a base where three lads, four lads, worked altogether and there used to be a big tool box, big enough for a lad to get in it. They used to say to a new lad, 'Get in this box and see if tha fits in.' And just while we put lid on and while you're in they used to wee through cracks and course like naturally you got wee all over ya. Then like you got out to roars of laughter and they thought it were great fun. It happened to me and all of us in turn. You just form a ring of good friends on a higher level than your schoolday friends.

It were another stage in your manhood when you went down the pit. It really was in every sense a man's world. You learnt a lot and you become a man because you were in a man's world. They're big swearers, big blasphemers while you're down the pit 'cos you're not offending anybody, there's no women, there was no children. They didn't think on us as children at fourteen, we were down pit and we were part of the environment. I've heard men swear for a quarter of an hour and not use same word twice.

At the weekend you got yer wages, thirty-five shilling then for five days, and you handed it over to your mum. It was a lot of money extra then and she give me half a crown which was the general thing.

It's surprising what wonders that half crown made to you. You'd started doing manly things and even at fourteen and fifteen we started slipping a little packet of fags in. Smoking looked big, that's why we started it in the first place. We thought it made us look big. And drinking, we thought, 'Oh, you're a big man if you can smoke and drink.'

They were big drinkers in that village. There were nowt else. It was a club life and pub life. They'd measure a man like and say, 'Oh, when he's had a coupla pints he's as daft as a brush.' Which meant to say he wasn't good at drinking but some of 'em could really 'old their drink, pints. If you could take your drink and not act stupid you were held in kind of, not esteem, but they'd say for instance, 'Look at him, he's had twelve pints and he can walk as straight as a die.'

I remember first time I went in a pub having this glass of beer and I remember 'ow me head was spinning like because I'd never drank before and they'd more or less to take me out after only a glass. But you get started getting used to it and you started supping a bit more till finally when you're getting up to seventeen you're supping at the rate of most. Bitter beer and mild.

There used to be a pub called Cross Daggers. This old lady kept this pub and we used to slip in there sometimes. Fourpence for a glass of beer and you thought you were manly supping, having a pint. The old lady used to come in sometimes and she used to say, 'How old are you?' We could fool her sometimes then odd occasion local bobby 'ud come in and he'd say, 'Right, you, you and you, out and don't let me ever catch you in 'ere again.' We used to keep out for about a month, then we used to trickle back.

We was an age when trilby 'ats was the thing and four of us went to Sheffield and bought these trilby 'ats. We'd been watching old films in them days. Most of them they were all trilby hat films, everybody, FBI and all, they all wore trilby hats. We all got 'em on at cocked angles like as if we was local film stars. We actually bought a pipe each and we bought this big tin of shag tobacco between us. We went to pub in evening and we was smoking pipes. Just one day that lasted 'cos we were all sick, we were all ill with pipes and we chucked them away next day. We kept trilbies for quite some while. It were a macho image with trilby.

There was a monkey run, they used to call it the prom, and we used to go Sunday night and pick girls up and have a glass of beer or a walk round, but nothing that stuck really, not in my case. When they got to work some on 'em would be boasting about the conquests. We all did the big man stuff when we were at work, boasting about us conquests and what we did and us sexual experiences which for the better part, for me, I never had. You knew they were telling lies, just boasting. They were trying to make theirself look big, as if they got a woman every time they walked out of door and they didn't at all.

Frank Davies

•

Frank started work as a probationary engineering apprentice at Metro-Vickers in Trafford Park in Manchester straight after his fourteenth birthday. Apart from his Second World War service he remained with the company until 1969 when he bought a newsagent's shop. He retired fully in 1982. Now he spends a lot of his spare time painting local scenes and wildlife, and his pictures decorate his house.

•

A quick, rushed breakfast and straight outside and you had to scramble on to a tram amongst all these big tough hobnailed boots characters all pushing and shoving. All the kids, as they used to call us, right to the front.

I'd never been in a factory in my life, never seen the inside of a workshop, and it was a really terrifying experience. One mad cacophony of noise and there were machines that you'd never even heard of, and people welding, belts flying round. It was just like another world all of a sudden.

Then they dumped you at the side of this foreman's desk and that was it. 'Right, put yer things on there, do this. How old are you, what's your name?' You were an errand lad. They'd write something on a piece of paper and you'd go to the stores and collect it. If you was slow they were all ready to shout at you. And while somebody was asking you to do something, another one would pin a thing on yer back and it used to say p'rhaps 'Pat me on the head' or a big L sign. And they're all patting you on the head, you know, until you found out. Others would send you all the way to the other end of the factory for a long stand. They'd give you a chitty with it written on, 'One long stand.' So you'd go to the storeman and you'd be stood there. It didn't dawn on you, you know, you were that green like. You would get sent there next for a bucket of steam, big tin buckets they were. Then you'd get brew time and you had to go round and collect all the cans, take all the brews all wrapped in greaseproof paper. Cocoa some had, coffee, tea, all wrapped in little bits of greaseproof paper with tinned milk so you had to make sure you got each one right, stagger back upstairs with them. All your clothes were soaking wet where you'd spilled them.

You were into a man's world all of a sudden but we was looked on

Frank Davies (left) in his late teens with one of his workmates from Metro-Vickers dressed in their best suits for a Saturday night out.

•

as kids still. If an adult was passing he'd kind of give us a slating for using the words you shouldn't be using. I even had to have a box to reach the vice, I was so small.

Your first wage packet was a big landmark. I remember reading me name written on it and thinking I'd really made it then. Me mam took it off me and she sort of hugged me, I'd done well for her. When you'd got through the first week or two of this you used to talk to lads who hadn't done it, some who used to be staying on at school till they was sixteen, and you used to be dead cocky about it. 'You don't know what life is, we're working now, I get a wage, I do this.' It gave you a feeling of superiority like. It was all part of the act, to show that you were one of the men at last.

You used to see the older lads who could order the pint and sink the pint one after the other and then 'course you had to join that kind of throng. You try it and drink a couple of pints and go away and bring the lot up. You couldn't cope with it, but you had to meet that standard, you had to keep at it. The first time I tasted it, the beer tasted bloody awful you know. I thought, 'How do they drink this stuff?' But gradually you get addicted to it and I ended up I could hold drink with anybody.

I remember starting to shave. We used to call it bum fluff in those days, like a silvery sheen all around your chin and we all compared. 'Hey, is mine growing?' You're kind of looking sideways and sure enough it started to grow, you know, this fine, shiny, silky hair and you called it a beard. Anyway you'd go home and tell your father like, 'What can I do about this? Can I borrow your razor?' Well, in those days me father's was a big cut-throat razor. He had a strap behind the kitchen door and his razor in a silver case. Anyway he says, 'Right, yes, you've got a bit of a beard, we'll start you off.' And he got us an old one sharpened up. 'Course I was well away but first few tries like I ended up with little bits of paper stuck all over my chin. But that was it, you could go out and tell your mates then, 'Oh I'm shaving now. Aren't you?' At least you were like growing up. You thought, 'I'm in the man's league now, I'm shaving.'

CHAPTER THREE

The Soldier

───────────●───────────

O n the morning of his nineteenth birthday Joe Yarwood, a
clerk in Clapham, South London, excitedly made his way to
the local recruiting office, knowing that he was now old
enough to volunteer for the British Army in the war against
Germany:

●

*I wanted to go and my time was up and I duly went along straight-
away, went to the town hall, and I was shocked unimaginably to think*

A recruiting poster from the First World
War. Pressure on young men to enlist and
prove their bravery was immense – conscription was not brought in until January
1916.

●

*they turned me down. 'Course as
far as I knew there was nothing
wrong with me except that I was a
bit skinny. I was over six feet tall
and I was fairly fit and they gave
me a total rejection, which I had to
accept. Then my firm put me out on
the road because some of their trav-
ellers had already gone and I went
to this place in Soho. When I
walked into the shop the woman
said, 'Why aren't you in the
army?' and in those days they'd
give you a white feather implying
that you were a coward, which I
definitely think I wasn't. So I said
'they've turned me down' and I
showed her the paper, total rejection,
and she said 'oh that's nonsense, go
to my brother who's a recruiting
sergeant in Whitehall and you'll
have no difficulty in getting in'. I*
*wasn't having any woman doubting my manhood so I went straight-
away and I found to my astonishment I got through quite easily.*

●

Two and a half million men volunteered for military service in the British Army during the first eighteen months of the First World War. The stampede to be a soldier was so great that in the early days the military aurthorities could be very selective about who they accepted. The men joined up for a combination of reasons: the promise of glory and adventure, the glamour of military uniform, the opportunity to escape from a monotonous job, fervent patriotism and solidarity with friends who were volunteering. This was most vividly expressed in the formation of hundreds of 'Pals Battalions' drawn from schools, neighbourhoods and towns like Salford or St Helens. Underlying all these motives was the deeply held belief that fighting for King and Country was a noble duty and the ultimate expression of manliness. This idea of manhood was reflected and reinforced in much war propaganda from the white feather campaign to recruiting slogans and posters like 'What Did You Do In The War Daddy?'

The testimony of men recruited at the beginning of the Second World War reveals a striking change in attitudes. Although some, like Frank Davies from Salford, still dreamed of military glory and heroic deeds many had a more realistic appraisal of what mass warfare was all about, based on the horrific experience of their parents' generation. The government – very aware of this sea change in attitudes – introduced conscription from the outset of the last war, recruiting young men like shy Bill Robertson from Bolton who had no desire whatsoever to be a soldier and who suffered terrible fear in battle. This new atmosphere, in which the war was viewed with apprehension rather than excitement, is remembered with sardonic humour by Alec Gunn.

•

I was called up and I had my medical in Northampton, which was very cursory. We just went before a doctor stark naked and he said 'cough' and that was just about it. Then I was called up to a drill hall in Sheffield on October 19th, 1939, and I went up with a suitcase with a whole lot of disconsolate young men in the pouring rain. We arrived at this very dreary drill hall, we went in and as we came in there was a very, very young officer with a cap that was too big for him which covered his ears and he took one look at us and he said 'Crumbs!' which I thought was a completely accurate description of our lot who came in.

•

The front line on the Somme, July 1916. The battle lasted for five months — soldiers had to live and fight in the trenches alongside the dead bodies of their fallen comrades.

•

Military training prepared young men for war: to obey orders, to use guns, to kill or be killed. In a sense they had been prepared since childhood with toy soldiers, cadets, boxing and books which celebrated Britain and her Empire. But nothing could really prepare officers and men for the mass carnage in the trenches which confronted them in the First World War. The initiation into the gruesome reality of death on the battlefield was deeply shocking. John Laister, a raw young recruit into the cavalry, recalls the savagery of hand-to-hand fighting and the decapitation which resulted from the use of swords and lances. The men quickly learned the limits to any compassion that could be shown for the dead and the dying. Joe Yarwood became a stretcher bearer in the Royal Army Medical Corps and remembers his first contact with death. 'The first case I carried out was a poor fellow shot through the head. Like a silly fool I felt sorry for him, I put my tunic under him and half his brains came out on it. Of course I had to have a new tunic and when the colonel heard about it he said "if you do it again you'll have to pay for the tunic".

The worst slaughter came in the huge battles of 1916–17. On the first day of the Somme in July 1916 there were 60 000 British casualties. In all during the battles of the Somme and Passchendaele around half a million British soldiers were seriously injured or killed. These were futile battles which led nowhere, fought in an extra-terrestrial landscape of mud and barbed wire, master-minded by generals who lived in comfort far behind the front line. That so many men could allow themselves to be used in this way as cannon fodder was in part due to the idea that the battlefield – however gruesome – provided a crucial test of manhood. Deep-rooted values of manliness also lay behind the regimental pride and camaraderie which were so important in helping to keep the men going. Traditions of honour, strength in adversity, brotherly love and a fearless attitude to danger and death formed the bedrock of army life and shaped the aspirations of the ordinary soldier during the First World War. This concern with manly courage was especially strong amongst officers. Leading their men over the top they suffered the highest casualty rate of all. Around one in five died. For officers like Richard Hawkins the duty to lead, to set a good example to the men and not to 'funk' were all-important and unquestioned. To be injured in battle was a badge of manhood as Norman Edwards, who rose to be an officer in the Gloucestershire

Regiment, remembers. For him trench warfare 'made a man of me, I think. You felt you'd done your duty. You had the satisfaction of knowing you'd not only done your duty, you'd been wounded doing it. You had a stripe on your arm which showed that you'd been wounded in action, you'd actually been in the front line.'

But as the number of casualties increased, more and more men in the ranks became preoccupied with survival rather than heroics. Ted Francis, who served with the Birmingham City Battalion, remembers the elaborate strategies he used when going over the top to ensure that he was not mowed down by machine-gun fire. A few deliberately wounded themselves – inflicting a 'Blighty wound' – that ensured a passage back to England. This, and any other action deemed to be cowardly, was punishable by death, the ultimate sanction which forced men to carry on fighting. Three hundred and forty-six British soldiers were executed during the First World War – John Laister recalls the horror of being in a firing squad ordered to shoot a former comrade.

What seems to have upset men most of all was the death of friends they had fought with over a long period. Sometimes they had to carry on in the presence of their dead and dismembered bodies. Joe Yarwood remembers how in one artillery attack in 1918, 'I lost two comrades, real comrades, fellows I was really fond of, decent blokes. One was Arthur Hartland, he was a varsity student from Widnes in Lancashire, he was killed, and so was dear old Wilf Uren, he was a church organist. And dear old Wilf, if we were in a village, if he could find a piano we'd have a tune for half an hour, with him playing and have a glass of French beer. There was poor Wilf lying on the deck dead, nice bloke he was, harmless, nothing vicious about him at all.'

In traumatic moments like this some looked to religion for support to keep up a show of courage and manliness that was so important in the front line. Joe Yarwood:

•

Sometimes you got so bad that you had the sort of runaway feeling, you can easily show it, but I hope I didn't anyway, I tried not to. I kidded myself I was a bit of a Christian and I always used to like to go to communion 'cos I thought it might help to ward it off. I mean any man with any guts doesn't want to feel like that, especially if he's going to show real cowardice, as is possible. And it was really rather romantic, 'cos you'd go to communion and there was the clergyman with his surplice and showing below would be his riding boots and spurs. It was always out in the open, you hadn't got a church, and he'd bring out the communion plate, all very rough and ready, but it was quite interesting and I was hoping I'd get some benefit from Him of course, that I wouldn't be showing the white feather.

•

In the last war religion served a similar function, even though there had been a gradual decline in Christian faith and observance following the First World War. Alec Gunn recounts, 'I'm a Christian believer, but I'm afraid my prayers were purely selfish. I just said "Oh God, get me through this war whole", whole being the operative word because I had a horror of being blinded. It was very selfish prayers but it did help, it did help a certain amount.'

The soldier in the last war was spared some of the horrors experienced by those who fought in the trenches during the First World War. There were improved conditions for the troops – partly because it was a more mobile war that didn't degenerate into the stalemate which claimed so many lives on the old Western Front. And there was greater regard for human life, resulting in far fewer casualties: almost three-quarters of a million British soldiers died in the First World War compared to less than 150 000 in the Second World War. But if he was captured by the enemy, the soldier in the last war was much more likely to be denied basic human rights, to be tortured or to be treated in a systematically brutal way. The Japanese – who believed that soldiers who surrendered were without honour – were responsible for some of the worst atrocities. Over a quarter of all British soldiers in Japanese POW camps died in captivity. One of the most appalling episodes in the treatment of British POWs was their use as slave labour to build the 300-mile Burmese railway through mountain and jungle. More than 6000 died, many from malnutrition and disease. Frank Davies still graphically remembers the terror of this ordeal and the profound impact it had on his identity as a young man.

Some of the most awful conditions and harrowing hand-to-hand fighting in the last war were experienced in the jungles of occupied Burma as Allied troops advanced against the Japanese. William de Silver was one of the Anglo-Burmese soldiers who acted as guides and saboteurs in the advance of the 'Chindits' (a name derived from the Burmese word for hen). His story is testimony to the important, yet often forgotten, role played by soldiers drawn from the Commonwealth and Empire – some of whom, like William, later emigrated to Britain.

Many soldiers who survived the two world wars look back on wartime as one of the most important and influential experiences of their life. The physical and psychological effects were, in the majority of cases, probably greatest for the men who fought in the First World War. In 1919 it was calculated that almost a quarter of a million British soldiers had suffered amputated arms or legs as a result of war wounds. Nevertheless for some, like Norman Edwards, the massive human cost of the war never led to a questioning of fundamental assumptions about manliness on the battlefield. 'I've been proud of being a member of the Glosters ever since, it was a very good regiment, their esprit de corps was first class in every way.'

But for many, especially those who were becoming disillusioned with the mass slaughter in the latter stages of the war, it was all a waste. Naïve, youthful ideals of manly courage were shattered. Ted Francis was so troubled by what he had gone through, he was unable to speak to anyone about his experiences on the front line for the rest of his forty-year working life.

Ted Francis

•

Now in his hundredth year, Ted Francis lives alone in a beautifully kept, semi-detached house in Solihull. His daughter, Norma, lives locally and is a great help to him, but he still maintains his independence. His large garden is his pride and joy, especially the chrysanthemums which he grows every year. When the First World War was declared he left his 'boring kind of job' at the paper factory, and joined Kitchener's Army in search of travel and adventure. He was posted to France where he joined his older brother Harry. They served together for most of the war.

•

When the war was declared I thought there would be a great adventure. I walked over to the Birmingham town hall intending to join the Army and I was amazed to see a long queue of

Men rush to join Kitchener's Army in 1914. During the first ten days of the recruitment campaign, 439 900 men had taken the King's Shilling and joined the forces. In the months that followed a further two and a half million were to volunteer.

•

laughing young men waiting to be soldiers.

It was more like a queue for a music-hall than to be a soldier. You'd have thought that an extra bank holiday had been told in Birmingham because people were that excited the day the war was declared. Laughing, joking, young people like myself were saying, 'We'll show those Germans, we'll push them back home, how dare they walk over little Belgium.' We were anxious to get to France to have a go at them. It was wild thoughts of young chaps who had no idea. And of course everyone was saying, 'oh it'll be over by Christmas.'

When I came home after I enlisted my mother and father, oh, they tore me off a strip. My mother, oh, she said, 'you little fool, don't you understand there's only thieves and vagabonds join the army? Go back and tell them that you've changed your mind and you're not going to join.'

I can't do that.' I says, 'I've made an oath and accepted the King's shilling and that's that.'

We was training for six or seven months' and we was enjoying ourselves, we had a three-months camp in tents at Malvern and it was more like a holiday than training for wars. The very fact of our troops

Ted Francis (top row, far left) *at an army camp in France. He served with one of the Birmingham Pals Battalions through the Battles of the Somme and Passchendaele.*

•

having a rough time and actually getting wounded and dying never entered our heads. We was enjoying ourselves.

When we put on khaki the same as the other soldiers and the same as the soldiers in France, we thought then that we was really made. Then came the great day when we was issued with rifles. Now we was all waiting for that and even more thrill was when we had real bullets to fire at a target. We cleaned and brushed and hogged our rifle and looked down and pretended to shoot one another. I was fortunate in the way that I'd used an airgun and a sporting gun very often with the consequence that I got full marks and passed the first-class shot.

I suppose I only felt a man when I joined up, became a soldier. Otherwise I was a giddy young youth who was up to everything people of my age would be and I never gave it a serious thought about being a man. But especially when I had a uniform and especially when I had a gun, then I felt a man.

When we got to France you could see some of 'em swelling up absolutely fit to bust with pride and I too. Being cheered by the French and mostly girls too. We thought it was great to be a soldier then. 'We'll show them.' It was just the thoughts of really young men who didn't know any better.

The first man in the company to be killed, it kind of sobered us up and in another day two or three was killed or wounded and it all came to our minds this was no outing, this was real. It kind of put a doubt about this soldier business. Here we was in the real thing, we were not playing at soldiers now, people were getting killed and we could hardly take it all in.

The first thing they do is to give you half a glass full of this rum and believe me when you had a half a glass full of that rum you'd take on the whole German Army itself. You felt that nothing could hurt you and you do the most silliest and bravest things ever. It was good in its way but it only lasted for so long and when it had worn off you was your old self again.

You see when you were over the top a whistle goes at a certain time and you were supposed to dash over. The man with the one stripe he was the first man to scramble up the top of the trench and say, 'Come on lads'. And in the second minute he's dying at the bottom of the trench, a machine-gun all to himself.

Now me and Harry who witnessed all this thought, 'That's ridiculous, I'm not going over the top on the sound of one whistle, I'm going over the top when the machine-gun passes the trench on to another. As it swerves round that's the time to get out.' So on the whistle we never got up but when the machine-gun was knocked off shooting the top of our trench up then we got up and dashed for the nearest shell hole. I put that to a great deal that we missed either being wounded or killed in the early stages.

Going over the top is not one straight line just marching or charging along. The line was broken, one in front, one behind, and at this particular time Corwyn was in front of us you see. And from our point in a shell hole we saw him get this terrible death blow and he fell down screaming.

And when you saw a friend who you had enlisted with and you'd come all this way and you were pals and all of a sudden he's struck down with a terrible wound – his leg half blown off and you are under instructions you can't go to him. His screams sometimes really I can hear now. The screams not for one hour but for several hours you could hear above everything else, even above the shell fire. Eventually, it was at least ten hours or more before they could get to him and by that time he'd slowly, his breath had failed and his wound had sunk into mud and water. He's left there, he's not gathered in because there are hundreds dead lying about and they have no time to mess with dead people. My friend left there, a half skeleton, eaten by rats.

That was really when we felt that we'd lost something that could never be put back. We'd lost a friend who for months and months had talked and laughed and joked and gone walks with us. There was a friend of ours years before he was hit.

As the years went on it was the same thing over and over again. 'We got to capture so and so village, we got to capture the farm, we got to capture their trench.' These route marches were sometimes very long. With a rifle and kit you was getting very tired and fed up. The officers were saying, 'Keep in step'. Then it would be, 'Let's have a song boys'. To buck us up as we was nearing a town or a village to march through. We was almost forced, it was an order, 'Sing you blighters, don't put your head down, stand up, march properly and sing.' It was something to impress other people, but it didn't impress us at all.

The main idea with Harry and I was keeping alive. We had no thoughts for practically any other people, there was only our skill and knowledge and being aware of the danger and not feeling frightened. In every attack there was men more frightened than others, who couldn't hold themselves, men who really had shell shock. Some of them really go absolutely mad, shrieking. They couldn't stand the tremendous fire and the shells and the noise. Everyone was afraid and as a matter of fact to see people who couldn't stand it made us a little bit more braver. We felt good that they couldn't stand this sort of thing but we could. That was the sort of feeling that made us go on and on and on.

Your first idea was if you could get out of going over the top. You felt that it was worth doing the very dangerous jobs because when it came to it a couple of times me and Harry would be rewarded by the officer saying we didn't have to go over the top. So when they asked for volunteers for a really dangerous job such as going over the top at night and inspecting their German wire, me and Harry was the first on the list. We was ready to do anything they wanted us to. You was afraid, but it's a kind of thing that once you get into and feel that up to now you haven't been hit, you're all right. The idea of being frightened has worn off you see.

I was offered a stripe but I said I wanted to remain a private. I wouldn't dream of telling a man to do something which I didn't do, to order him to do something that he got killed when doing it. That would be on my conscience a long time and I was unfit to do that. So although they pressed me I refused any promotion.

Life was cheap, two-a-penny. It didn't matter how many men were killed or wounded as long as they attained a German trench. It happened many a time that we held it for half a dozen hours till they came back at us about twice or three times and drove us back to where we originally started. All lives were thrown away uselessly.

When we came to the Somme tens of thousands of shells had been sent over to the German line and the day before we was supposed to go over the top a high ranking officer come down to our lines. He got off his horse and said to us, 'Tomorrow men, you go and take the German trench. There's no wire there, it's all been pounded by our guns and you can just walk over and carry your guns as you would carry a bag.' He wished us good luck and all the rest. I said to Harry, 'What does he know about it? He don't come any nearer than thirty miles from the trench.'

And of course it cost thousands of lives for that foolish officer saying that. The wire was still there and the Germans was still there in fifteen-foot dugouts that they had built. Their machine-guns picked off our men as easy as anything because they was doing as they were told, just strolling over to the trench. You saw the sights, men blown to pieces, men with terrible wounds in the legs who are slipping in water, who are crying out terrible and we daren't under strict orders to go to them. Thousands was killed like it, foolish words.

Passchendaele was the most terrible conditions. We'd had frost, we'd had rain and everywhere you went it was mud and water. We was standing in water above our knees. You'd got to walk around in the pitch black trying to keep your rifle out of the mud and you'd got to be very careful as when two shell holes nearly met. You saw many a poor fellow met his death through a simple thing like that.

We was absolutely exhausted and it was only then that I was at a very low ebb, as was everybody and we cursed the Army for all its worth. You was always thirsty, occasionally you'd get water in a petrol tin that tasted of petrol. You'd got to rely on biscuits that was hard as rock and you was always sleepy. Sleep was out of the question. Only if you could stagger out of some action the first thing you did was sleep and you slept for twenty-four hours provided the rats didn't bite yer nose.

The rats got so many and they grew that they was not frightened. They'd come in the daylight in the trench and look up at you. They wouldn't run away unless you put the boot behind them. And every month and every year the rats grew more and more. Harry and I thought, 'Well why is the rats growing?' And it suddenly dawned upon us that the rats were eating the dead men. These rats in a few nights would reduce a body to skeleton.

Everybody was looking for a Blighty one and it only very rarely came. They didn't want a wound that lost a leg or an arm which was more likely than a small wound that got you home.

I was off duty and I was told to go to a little dug-out to sleep for two hours. I must have been sound asleep when the shell hit. If it had been one of the big shells of course I shouldn't have been here today but it was a whizz bang as we'd call them. It blew the top and all them bits and pieces of iron on top of me leg. All that lot fell with some shrapnel on me leg and I screamed with pain.

A lot of us in hospital couldn't realize that with our wounds we'd never go back to the Front again. That was always the fear in men that was lightly wounded, the fear that they told the nurses, they told the doctor, 'Oh I can't go back to the Front again I can't stand that again. Please tell 'em that I'm not fit for the trenches again.'

When the doctor says I'd have to be removed to England, those was the words that for four years I'd longed to hear. I could have kissed him and however painful my ankle was didn't matter. I couldn't believe it until I'd crossed the Channel.

I did think of my childish dreams of gallant deeds by men on horses that I'd read about and I did think, 'Oh what a fool I was to take all that in'. If there's anyone detested the Army in the last months or so it was me. At the time I liked a little monologue about the war that I used to recite to me pals and I've remembered it ever since. It reminds me of my friends, good pals I lost out there.

Spotty was my pal he was, a ginger-headed bloke,
An everlasting gas bag and as stubborn as a moke.
He gave us all the 'ump he did afore it came to war,
By sporting all his bits of French what no one asked him for.
Where we went to nobody knows,

The Soldier

And it wasn't like the fighting that is seen in picture shows.
We had days of hell together till they told us to retire
And Spotty's floral language set the water carts on fire.
But him and me was very lucky for two-thirds of us were dead,
With the screaming Black Marias and the shrapnel overhead.
But every time they missed us and their fire was murderous hot
But Spotty shouts, 'Encore, encore'. I said, 'What's that?'
He said, 'It's French for rotten shot.'
We were lying down in a 'ole, yes dug with our very hands
For you gets it quick and sudden if you moves about or stands.
We was sharing half a fag, yes turn and turn about.
When I felt him move towards me and he said, 'Old mate, I'm out.'
His eyes they couldn't see me, nor never will no more
And his twisted mouth just whispered, 'So long matey, au revoir.'
But there was none quite the same to me 'cos him and me were pals
And if I could have him back again huh you could keep your fancy gals.
But he's talking French in heaven now so it's no use feeling sore
But God knows, how I miss him, so long Spotty, au revoir.

A dead British soldier in a trench near Guillemont on the Somme in 1916. He was one of
the 415 000 British casualties of the 142-day battle.

•

78

John Laister

•

John is a tiny, white-haired man with twinkling eyes. He lives in a sheltered housing block on the outskirts of Birmingham, the city where he has spent most of his life. The small room where he sits is dominated by a large piano. A violin lies on the piano stool, and photographs of the children he still teaches stand on the sideboard. He is animated when he tells his story, anxious to give the correct account with all the details in exactly the right order. Eighty years on and the terrible events of 1914–18 are burnt into his mind, as vivid as if they happened yester-day. He is haunted by a photographic memory.

•

John Laister in the 1920s. Like many ex-soldiers returning to 'A Land Fit for Heroes', John found himself without work. He was forced to try and earn a living by busking in the streets of Bermingham.

•

The officer says, 'Put him in the Lancers.' He said, 'They're not doing too good, put him in the Lancers.' I remember the trooper coming and collecting me, he says, 'Little ain't ya? Ah,' he says, 'I'll bet you'll be as good as the bloody big 'uns, come with me we'll get you a horse first.'

I didn't know one end of a horse from the other. We go down there and there's two or three 'orses all looking over the top of the stable. 'There you are, she's just right for you,' he said, 'Queenie.'

Well, what they did is they have sandbags rigged up on scaffolding, right, and you'd got to go at full gallop, shouting, 'ooh, ooh,' and then you practise your sword. You've got to swing it round your head to keep the Germans at a distance. Then you drive the lance into the person and when you get it in you must twist to let the air in the body else you won't get the lance out. Well that's that, that's your training.

Queenie was a wonderful 'orse. We used to have to get our 'orse to lie down and we 'ad it as a pillow. She'd got wonderful brown eyes, big eyes. I took a real liking to the 'orse, you know, after what I'd gone through in training with her. Learning about snaffle bits and saddles and all that. I thought it'd break me heart if I didn't get through and I were really surprised I did 'cos I'm only five foot and a half.

When we got out to France we went as an advanced patrol, because they didn't know where the Germans were. We were riding in pairs, that's twenty of us. Jock was riding on the right of me. He said to me, 'Have you made your will out? D'you know they told us to in the back page of your paybook?' I said, 'No. I didn't know what to put.' So he said he'd left everything to his mother. And that's the talk when we're going down this lane.

We're going along and Jock's singing, 'Ye take the high road and I'll take the low road.' And all of a sudden we see a lance, a tip of a lance, coming round the corner of the lane and the sound of horses' hooves. And a German appears with skull and crossbones and all that and he nearly pulled his horse on to his haunches to turn round. We 'eard him galloping away and the Squad says, 'Quiet, the main body won't be far away. Now you must pick what you're going to use, your lance or your sword.' Well the sword was a terrific weight for me and I thought I'll cut the top of me 'ead off or something like that, so I decided on the lance.

Eventually we set off at a steady gallop and that's when I found the strap on the lance was rubbing the skin, through the wind resistance, and I was so sore I couldn't feel me legs.

I'll never forget this, we're riding along he said, 'Go on, advance'. And all of a sudden the lane ends and there's a big ploughed field, and perhaps fifty yards away is a squadron of German cavalry, with the skull and crossbones in chrome, shining in the sun, and before we knew where we was they galloped towards us and we spread out and I levelled the lance almost level with Queenie's ear. This German or whatever he was coming towards me and I pulled the 'orse up and the lance went straight through him.

I hadn't got the strength to pull the lance out, so the squadron leader's galloping past and I'm dragging this German along, at full gallop. 'Take the strap off yer lance and leave the bastard with the lance,' he shouts at me. And that's what I did. Then no sooner I'd done that there was another German coming for me from the other

British Cavalry riding through Achicourt in 1917.
Even at that time the cavalry was seen as an outdated method of warfare,
although General Haig insisted on including them in his battle strategy.

•

side. He cut a lump out of Queenie's shoulder, it was running with blood and I was covered with white lather and blood. See, when the horses are in a cavalry charge they're like mad things. You can keep pulling but you can't pull their head over and she was going like hell, like a mad thing. And I could see this other German making for Jock and I couldn't pull Queenie over to that side and I saw Jock's head cut clean off.

When I got through to the end of this field I got off the 'orse and I looked into her big brown eyes and she seemed to say to me, 'What have you done to me, my God, what have you done to me?' Then I've got to thread my way through these dead and dying and I'd get one man jumping up and grabbing me then falling down again. I would have loved a swift death then, I would have loved it. To get rid of all the misery. I was sore, I was sick, I could hardly walk. I just wanted to die. We'll never see Blighty again, and we're finished.

Squad came and he says, 'That was a bloody fight wasn't it.' But I couldn't speak properly, I could hardly walk and I was sick. I wanted to die, I wanted a quick death. 'My God,' I thought, 'the world's gone mad, that's it.'

After the cavalry charge John Laister was transferred to the infantry for the remainder of the war.

When we got back to the base as a rule the orderly corporal comes round with the orders for the next day and this one time he says, 'I'll be coming to collect so many of your rifles later.' Well I didn't know what it was for and I thought it was funny, taking our rifles. Then they brought 'em back, for six of us, see.

So the next thing was we were to parade at four o'clock in the morning. It's a funny feeling, even now, I can picture the six of us lined up there and this bit of a kid. It's just breaking daylight, right, we marched into the wood. We know what we're on now, firing squad, and we wait quite a while and all of a sudden there's two military police, one on each arm leading – you don't know whether they're leading him or whether they're bloody dragging him, 'cos it's semi-darkness and they prop him up and they say to him, 'Want a blindfold?' And they put the blindfold on him. I felt sorry for him, terribly sorry. And I never asked for tears to come in my eyes. Then they told us to aim, fire.

Cowardice, that's why they said they sentenced him to death. That kid's no coward, just a bundle of nerves. It could happen to anyone – it could happen to me. I kept saying to meself, 'You haven't shot him, you know.' I kept saying that.

Well this plays on my mind sometimes, sometimes I can't sleep. I've gone all through the war, but all of a sudden, when I'm in bed, something will crop up, so I see every detail, that's the damn trouble, see.

Richard Hawkins

•

Richard Hawkins died in his hundredth year, 1994. He thought ninety-nine was an 'indecent age' to be. He had volunteered to fight for his country as soon as the Great War was declared, leaving his home in

*Chelmsford, Essex, and joining one of the public schools' battalions –
the 11th Service Battalion of the Royal Fusiliers. Sitting in his chair,
looking back through his leather-bound photo albums and letters written from the trenches, he often thought about the friends he lost during
those years. He was described by many who knew him as 'very much
an officer and a gentleman'. He read the* Telegraph *daily, marking
with a red pen any points for discussion and, although confined to a
wheelchair, he dominated the retirement home where he spent the last
of his days.*

•

*Richard Hawkins photographed in 1914
shortly before he left for France as a young
officer with the 11th Service Battalion of
the Royal Fusiliers.*

•

You had a damn good father
and a damn good mother
and you just did as you were told,
that's all. My mother was perhaps
a little bit of a martinet, like
Queen Alexandra, but my father
was too busy arranging concerts
and shows in the Shire Hall to get
money for his good deeds. What
he did for the accountancy company as the chief accountant I
never quite knew. Paid the wages
on Friday I should think.

And I went to a decent school
which had a cadet corps and that's
where we learned for the future
largely. When I was twelve I was
the sergeant of number something
section and there was no question,
the other boys had to do as I told
them. My goodness me, yes, rather.
We went out on manoeuvres and
some regular officers from the War
Office would very often come down and watch these manoeuvres.
We took it very seriously and we enjoyed it. Occasionally I got
immeasurably 'wounded' early in the day and went to sleep in the
field and the battle would go on, but never mind. It made a difference, I would say, to the whole of one's life.

One has behaved oneself, the whole of one, because of that early training.

And this country ruled the British Empire and the British Empire ruled the world. I mean, we were the best country in the world, the best everything in the world, we were all very proud of ourselves. There wasn't anywhere else. We knew about Europe and the French and the Italians and things and so on, but I don't think we ever gave it any thought, there was no need to, we were better than anybody else and that's why I think Kitchener had no difficulty in finding a hundred thousand men to go and defend it against all invaders and to give, if necessary, our lives to do it. No trouble about it, perfectly normal.

It was my duty and the duty of every young man to join up. Dammit, you couldn't get into the ruddy army there was such a rush to get there, to get on, and defeat the enemy.

We were given a grant of thirty pounds for our uniforms and we had to buy our own revolver for three quid. I had a lovely big Webley. Well, we were the best battalion, there was no better. We were very proud of ourselves, built up by discipline. Once we had the uniform on, we weren't conceited but it was a question of if there wasn't room on the pavement, he would have to get off and not me, sort of thing. The morale was tremendous.

All nice, decent blokes. We all had great fun really, tremendous fun, enjoyed ourselves. I personally enjoyed the ruddy war. It wasn't very pleasant to see others being thrown up in the air, and watch the great big five-gallon shells. 'Where's that going to drop, now which way do we run?' Don't you know, and we didn't think about any of the other. Damn good lot of chaps behind us and behave ourselves, set them an example.

Well, you got to make sure they were washed behind their ears, you see. And why the hell they did as they were told by a young man, probably younger than they were, I don't quite know except that they were told that I was in charge of them, that I was the officer, no question of it.

As the time went on they were wounded or killed and perhaps they weren't such good types left. It was all very sad, but there was a hell of a war going on and you'd got to get on with it. You were there despite you might be wounded or killed at any moment yourself. The Hun was throwing things at you all day long, or all night long very often and I don't think you gave it very much thought. You'd get on with the job, that's all. Another big battle was on the way and you hadn't got time – 'Sorry old thing, very sorry, poor old so-and-so being killed, damned bad luck, never mind, can't help it. Let's get on boys, let's get on with the job.' People were being killed all day long.

I went round with the rum bottle every morning at dawn, round the trenches, and the tot was an eighth of a pint. You could feel that rum going down into your boots which were probably full of icy water, drying up the water, coming up to you and saying, 'Now where's that ruddy Hun?' It saved lives. Old Navy Rum, until supplies ran out and then we got ordinary rum, by Jove, there was a lot of difference. But with that old Navy stuff one would have taken on the whole of Germany at dawn in the morning, and I don't exaggerate about that. Unhappily I had one of the best company sergeant majors that ever was but one day he went too far and had too much and had to be sent home. Very sad.

On the Somme, first day of the battle, we moved up into our front-line trench. Every man was given a packet of Woodbines. Stupid thing to say, but I went over smoking an Abdullah, a sort of oval cigarette. Zero hour was seven thirty, it was a lovely morning and over the top we went. Actually we had a very good day. The Manchesters on our right were held up and somebody else on our left was held up and that's why we had to stop really, otherwise some idiot said we would have walked straight through to Berlin. I had to leave my batman. I thought he was dying and I had to leave him for dead. I'd got to get on with the war but he got away with it, he was all right. Grand fellow, fellow called Good. As I say he was wounded on the 1st July. We were great friends, damn good chap.

General Maxie came to see us a few days afterwards and said, 'Gentlemen, damn good show, thank you very much, you did very well, marvellous.'

I'd had a shell which landed, literally at my feet, but it didn't go off and that caused me to be a bit muzzy for the time being but anyway I spent the night down in the cellar of the château, what was left of it. Colonel Maxwell was there, been in some previous war, no idea of fear. He didn't understand the word fear at all and he enjoyed every moment of the war. One of the boys sitting down there had a bit of shell shock and he kept running around. Maxwell said, 'Give him a damn good kick up the backside as he passes you, he'll be all right.'

Richard Hawkins in a trench on the Somme.
This photograph was taken with Richard's small VPK camera
which he had to keep hidden during his time at the front.
Taking photographs in the trenches was strictly against
army regulations.

•

And he was, he was all right. That's the sort of chap Maxie was.

He said to my colonel one day, he said, 'You know Carr, I don't think you really enjoy this war, do you?'

Carr said, 'My God, I do not, I think it's a dreadful business.'

And Maxie said, 'I think it's marvellous, I thoroughly enjoy it.'

That's absolutely true and he did and eventually he was promoted to Brigadier and was killed walking over the top. As a brigadier he shouldn't have been walking over the top at all, he should have been behind at his headquarters but he just couldn't keep out of it.

Boom Ravine was the big one we'd got to take. Early morning we went along the line with the rum bottle, we gave all the chaps a tot of rum and waited for seven thirty when the barrage would open. Just before our barrage was due to come down the Hun put a barrage on us, somebody had given the show away probably. It was very unpleasant because we were being shelled to blazes. I said to Collis, 'Look this is going to be a dirty business.' And then something hit me in the shoulder and spun me round and I fell to the bottom of this ravine. It was very unpleasant. And there I stayed. The battle went forward to Boom Ravine and I must have gone asleep or became unconscious for the next thing I heard was, 'Cor blimey, 'ere's Captain Hawkins, poor so-and-so's dead.' I said, 'No I'm not but I shall be if you don't get me out of this lot.'

It had frozen for about four weeks, that night it thawed. The state of mud and icy water is beyond all description, so they got me on to the stretcher and took me back to the dressing station. And that was that and I woke up next morning very, very well and the doctor had kindly pinned the bit of shrapnel with a bit of cotton wool on to my pyjamas.

That was the end of my war. I was taken to No 14 Great Stanhope Street where one of the dearest women I've ever met had six of us to look after. Beautiful home. She looked after us and we lived, I'm ashamed to say, better than any royalty has ever lived.

They were a lot of damn nice fellows and, as I said, being fed beautifully and being looked after, taken up to the homoeopathic massage, up on the cliffs at Eastbourne, for treatment. I was ordered to play tennis on the tennis courts at Eastbourne, to exercise this shoulder. We were thoroughly spoilt, dear soul.

I was very glad. Nineteen months in the trenches is too long. Of course, you couldn't help being a bit frightened in battles, I think, but you couldn't show it, got to bottle it up. That's what ruined my digestive system really and my nervous system for a good many years afterwards. It was a great strain on me because I became Sales and Advertising Director of a Birmingham company and had to attend meetings and if I'd got to say something I could do it, I didn't actually stammer, but it was a frightful job to get started, a tremendous strain. I didn't sleep until three or four o'clock in the morning and used to go up through the ceiling and down again, dreadful business. It was a personal thing, nobody knew about it really, but it was a strain to hide it.

Bill Robertson

•

Bill lives with his wife Auriol in an orderly, semi-detached, inter-war house in Bolton. A retired painter and decorator he was nervous of being interviewed about his Second World War experiences. Since retiring he spent seven years working as a church warden in his local parish church, St Bede's, in Bolton. He has recently given up this role due to ill health, but the church remains very important to him.

•

Bill Robertson aged twenty at the start of the Second World War. He was sent to France in March 1940 with the Second Battalion of the Lancashire Fusiliers.

•

I was a very quiet lad, I was a choirboy, I didn't smoke, I didn't drink, I didn't gamble, and I was really immature. Then I had to register for the militia. You were going to have to go anyway so I had no choice. It gave me a fluttering in me stomach, a terrible depression. When it came to it I was given three days to sort everything out and get to the barracks. I thought, 'All me liberty's gone now.'

When I told the sergeant I didn't play cards, I didn't drink, I didn't gamble and I didn't swear he says, 'Well, what d'you do besides tell lies?' Because he didn't sort of believe me. But I wasn't compatible with these soldiers and they referred to me as 'he' and 'him' you know, never a name. And there we were all off to France together.

The first confrontation, the lieutenant gave an order out. He said, 'Now if the Germans attack, walking wounded make their way back, badly wounded must stay here. Leave them as they are.' He said, 'You know a dead man isn't as much trouble as a wounded man.' So these soldiers got together when he'd gone. 'We're not obeying that order.' They agreed between themselves that should one of them get wounded the others would help, whether or not, but they didn't consult me so I didn't know how I would fit in. I felt as if I was on me own.

The Germans sent some shells over, burst into smoke, and then they started attacking. The first shell dropped in this trench where Wilson and Dixon was and killed them outright. This was the trench that I'd just been moved out of and a piece of shrapnel came out off the same shell and dropped on my hand, and it was red hot, and I'd a piece stuck in my face, too, so it was as near as I could ever get to it really. Then I saw a balloon coming forward with a basket underneath from the Germans. I could see the Germans a long way off, and then a German plane kept dragging over the top of the trenches and I got a bit panicky, didn't know what was happening. When the barrage slackened off a little bit I ran to the house behind our lines and another man followed me, called Bushell. We ran down to the cellar and there was just Captain Hodson. He were very calm. Bushell shouted Dixon and Wilson were both dead. Then the Germans hit the house and all the side of the house came down. I was really panicking and me teeth was chattering like I bet you could hear them. So I picked a piece of rag up and it was dirty, I ripped it up and I folded it and stuck it in my mouth. I bit it all the time.

I was terrified. At times I thought about at home, what it would be like, what would be going on at home. I didn't know what I were doing and I didn't care what happened to me, I was so sort of shocked about it all, you know. I kept thinking about people at home and … I said me prayers.

When the officer got us all together he said, 'We're going to Dunkirk and a ship will pick us up and we're all going home.' It was good news but hardly believable really, what a relief. Then a German plane came over and it dropped leaflets and it said, 'British soldiers, you are cut off, lay down your arms and surrender.' And it showed a map. So the CO said to us, he said, 'You know this is true, this leaflet.' I can see him now at the end of that wood, he was drawing patterns with his toe and he said, 'Men, you've fought well and we are cut off and we have to escape. I want you to throw all the things away that you don't require, just carry yer rifles and ammunition. As you go along the road you might be bombed and shelled, or machine-gunned. It's going to be terrible for you. It looks a case of death or prisoner of war and you're better being dead then you've nothing to

Shocked and exhausted British soldiers at the evacuation of Dunkirk in May 1940.

worry about.' He was killed later that day.

All the men and the officers were pulling photographs out of their wives and children and we moved off. Before we set off we burned everything, destroyed all the rations and respirators, terrible destruction.

The captain wanted three men to go ahead on a patrol. Two volunteered. When he asked another one he said, 'Well I'm married and I've a family, I'm not risking it.' I found out the ones that was putting a brave face on cracked up first. It was much better being like I was, I couldn't crack up completely because I'd already been cracking up all the time, you know. So he come to me and he said, 'Are you married?' And I said I hadn't even been with a girl. But he says, 'I don't want a new recruit, I want a soldier.' He turned to another bloke and he said, 'What's wrong with you Pollard, are you man or mouse?'

Pollard said, 'Oh I'm a mouse.'

The captain says, 'Makes no difference, you're still coming.' So he took him.

We went along this road to a place called Bray Dunes. It was all sand and the Navy was shelling from the sea. But we never saw an aeroplane, nor a tank, or anything, not even artillery. We'd nothing to support us, just bren-guns and rifles. There was no defence at all against the Germans, it were like fighting with our hands behind our backs. There was a hospital nearby, evacuated. We went and got some bedding and blankets and made use of it and then we was told to make our way to Les Pains.

We walked along the front and there was quite a lot of dead civilians, some even children. They were on the pavement, and we just walked. Some of the houses had white flags flying, well we didn't like that, you know, surrender flags. They told us there were so many spies there. They wanted us to walk like civilians, in twos and threes and don't walk in step. We got to Les Pains and then they disappeared, the NCOs and officers. It were more or less every man for himself.

I followed a few soldiers and went down into a cellar and fell asleep and at dawn an officer came, with a lamp, like a Florence Nightingale lamp, and he said 'Men,' he said, 'I must warn you if you sleep on you'll be a prisoner in the morning. If you make a run for it you could be home.' So after a minute one got up, then another and I went on the front then.

There's queues to go into the sea, and the first queue I went to the officer said, 'This is Guards only'. He didn't want the queue too big 'cos he wanted to get away. He told me to find my own regiment. Well, we'd already split up so I walked in despair along the edge of the sea and I heard some shouting in a rowing boat. Because I was in between queues I was the only one as heard 'em. So I went out and they asked me to push them off the sandbank. I pushed this boat off and I fell in the water so they said. 'Oh, come on we'll give you a lift.'

Now the Navy at this point was shelling over the enemy. As far as I could see that was the only thing that was keeping the enemy away. They seemed to be big heavy shells what they were sending over all the time.

When I got back to Bolton there was flags out and folk waiting and I came to the conclusion that I was the only one in that little district that was away, because I had friends that I never knew I had coming to me and asking me and giving me money and all that sort of thing. I had two good days at home to reminisce and talk about it.

I said to Mother I said, 'You couldn't believe it mother, but I'm no soldier. I had diarrhoea, frightened in me stomach all the time, till I come home. I've never been as scared as that.' Mother said it was only natural but I thought it was a bit of cowardice, but that's how I felt all the time.

Oh and it always upset me going back. I think the closest to tears I used to get was walking down the lobby out of our home, out of the house where I lived all my life with me mother and father and that. Even one of me workmates, he was too old for the war, he was coming to see me off and shaking me hands. Our Barbara used to come and see me back on the train and the train moved off and I used to think, 'I wonder if I'll ever see this place again.' It were always like that, wondering if I'd ever get back.

William de Silver

•

He was born in 1924 in Mok Palin, a town on the Setang river in Burma. His parents were well-known figures in the Anglo-Burmese community, and he had ten brothers and sisters. William's mother and father moved to England in the 1950s, and William followed them

William de Silver in 1946 shortly after he was demobbed from the Burma Intelligence Corps.

•

and settled here in 1960. He is married to Isabel, an Anglo-Burmese teacher, and they live in a village outside Windsor. Since William retired from his job as Parts Manager at Peugeot in 1987 they spend a lot of time travelling together.

•

A friend of mine and myself decided that we will make an impression now on these girls, we got to pull the girls somehow, so we'll go, join up in the Army as a volunteer. You know, auxiliary force. We went down to the recruiting office and lied about our ages. I was sixteen then so to make it more definite I said I was nineteen years old and so did my friend.

We were shown how to march and how to drill with a rifle, things like that and we were given uniforms. Every Tuesday we would go to school in this uniform and from school we would attend parade. I think we made quite an impression in school, you know, soldier boys for that one day.

This carried on to when the Japanese first bombed Rangoon, 23rd December, 1941. A military sergeant rolled up at my place and said, 'Now come on, you're a volunteer, you're in the Army.' It was really a shock. I never realized what I had let myself in for. What the devil have I gone and done now? I was too afraid to run away, in those days you'd be shot as a deserter, you were liable to go to the firing squad. I think a lot of us soldiers were brainwashed. You didn't question, you were told you had to do that and you had to carry it out. You couldn't question it. Discipline was instilled in you.

After the fall of Burma we had to trek out to India and join the Burma Intelligence Corps for a period of jungle training. Then we were told that we were going to see some action.

We got on to these Dakotas, no seats or anything. We just had to sit on the floor with our little pack. All you had to take with you was one ground sheet, a pack with rations in it, lightweight blanket and your battle shorts and shirt, boots. We came down in this paddy field in Burma, wave after wave of Dakotas flying in continuously.

Immediately on getting off the plane I remember I got down on my knees, I kissed the ground. I collected a bit of the soil which I carried for years with me in my wallet. And I thought, 'This is my land, this is where I was born, this is my land and I love it.'

We had to scatter immediately, get off the airfields and there it was, action. Getting behind the Japanese lines.

In the old days, I mean pre-war, we always looked up to the British and they were considered sort of gods on a different plain to ourselves. But the Chindits in the jungles, we were all very much on a very equal level. I think they respected me and I respected them and we were great comrades.

I felt I could always depend on the next person, it gave me courage because they were going through the same thing as I was. We gained strength from each other's company and it helped you to get over the terrible fear. We got over it, somehow, I don't know how.

I didn't think, 'I'm fighting for King and Country.' But I did feel that the sooner it was over the sooner I would see my folks again, that's right. Dad and Mum and brothers and sisters, the sooner we would get together. I'd had no knowledge whether they were alive or dead but I always felt that they were alive and that the sooner I got to them the better.

My job was going out with the forward patrols, a section of about ten to fifteen men. We would go out ahead of the main body to gain knowledge about the Japanese. We were continuously marching, moving, patrolling, all the time. You often had to walk through streams, water right up to your neck and you would hold your rifles above your head.

You had one pair of trousers and one shirt and you lived in that, slept in that, ate in that, did everything in that. It was the monsoons and you were soaking wet day in and day out, soaked to the skin. You had to sleep very often in water, you were so tired you just slept in that water and you got up in that water. I remember once where we were marching up a hill and there was no water close by. The only water there was in a hole made by wild elephants that had walked through the path and left these big holes and water had collected in them. It was all muddy, dirty water and that was the only water that you collected, tried to strain it the best you could, and drank it. You had to, you were so thirsty. We all had water bottles but had not a drop left.

You could cover maybe twenty-five, thirty miles a day going through Japanese territory trying to find where the Japanese were and what damage we could do to them. We would form an ambush, lay in wait for them and we fired on them as soon as we saw them and after it was all over there would be a certain amount killed. It was just a case of kill or be killed. There was no option. You could not take a prisoner because for the simple reason you didn't have the spare food to feed him or take him with you. I think it was just a case of a job done, something had to be done and we had done it. I don't think I had many feelings at all.

There was a terrible fear being in the jungle that if you were shot you were liable to be left back because you were a burden to other people to carry you. I often felt that if I was shot in the leg I might just as well be shot in the head because that would be a better way for me to go out rather than be left behind and fend for myself.

I would be lost, no one would know. My parents wouldn't know, nobody would know. I would just be left there probably buried in the jungle over there completely forgotten. These fears all go through your mind. Who will know who I am? That I was killed over there, that I was buried over there. Would my parents ever be notified? I suppose we all had our tags but I just didn't want to be lost forever, you know, without any proper burial.

Before I went to sleep in the jungle I would make sure that I was sleeping on my back with only my boots pointing up. I sort of thought the metal studs in the boots would sort of save me if I should be shot at during the night. The bullets would not penetrate but would hit the metal studs and I would be safe. That was one of the superstitions before I went to sleep.

I would make sure that I didn't put my arms by my side or anywhere else. I said my prayers and folded my arms across my chest and that for some reason would keep me safe. That was a terrible superstition that. I felt perhaps like someone was hugging me.

Even when I went to sleep I had to have this dagger with me. It had a horn handle and a blade about six inches long in a sheath. I always felt that this would somehow keep me safe from being captured or shot or injured. What I was going to do with that I don't know. Perhaps if I got too close to an enemy or he was just going to take me perhaps I could kill him with this dagger. It was a lucky charm with which I would beat the forces of evil somehow.

You sort of conquered that fear because you were afraid, I think, to show fear. I didn't want anybody to look down on me. I wasn't exactly afraid to show that I was frightened, not that I'm brave or anything like that, but you couldn't do anything about it. I suppose it was pointless trying to show that you were frightened, you just had to go through with it. You couldn't run away from it, you couldn't hide from it, it was there and you just had to face it. There was nowhere to hide.

Frank Davies

•

When the Second World War was declared Frank wanted to join the Yeomanry, something glamorous and heroic. The recruiting officer suggested that with his technical apprenticeship background he would be better off in the Royal Army Ordnance Corps. His age prevented him being sent abroad straightaway, so it was 1941 before he was finally sent on active service overseas. His experiences in a Japanese POW camp still affect him deeply. He is involved with the organization for Far Eastern Prisoners of War, FEPOW.

•

There were lads walking round with these fancy uniforms. To me they looked like heroes and that's what I wanted to be. I wanted a crack at being a soldier hero and so I went off to join up.

Word had got round, this young hero's going to war, you know, and all the neighbours from our street were all waving to me and patting me on the back, giving you cigarettes, chocolates and waving you off as a hero. I lapped it all up like and off I went.

We kicked our heels in England with some anti-aircraft batteries and we ended up seeing quite a bit of action in this country in the Coventry Blitz, Birmingham, Liverpool. But eventually we joined this artillery mob that were equipped to go and guard the pipe-lines in the Middle East there, and all your kit was made sand colour.

*Frank Davies in the army uniform he was so proud of
with his sister Evelyn
shortly after he joined up in 1940.*

•

We were half-way there when the trouble started with Japan so they diverted us and dumped us in Singapore. We weren't equipped for that area, wrong colour uniform and all. We had never heard of jungle, we didn't know what it was all about. We'd never heard of Malaya or Singapore, but suddenly that was it, you were there and it was utter chaos.

I always remember this sergeant major, he was telling us, 'Now the Japs are all short-sighted. You'll find most of 'em wear thick glasses so when it goes dark they can't see at all. Don't worry about it lads, if you see one he can walk up to you but he won't know you're there.' It was all codswallop. They told us that the power was that low in the cartridges they used that you could pull the bullets out with a pair of pinchers. But we lapped this up.

After a month or two of not knowing what the hell we were doing, we were just a rabble wandering about Singapore wondering where yer destiny was. We'd nothing to fight. We'd nothing to kind of back us up. We all had to be gradually squeezed into the island of Singapore, there was no way out, and we took over an old engineering firm, right in the centre somewhere. We took this as a final stand you know and we made it into some form of a garrison, sandbagged it and made gun positions.

The Japs were closing in, they were shelling from the sea, mortaring from the air, they were machine-gunning. We were getting the lot, dive-bombed, and the officer came in and told us that this was your last stand and he wants you all to die like true Britons. All that did was put the fear of God up us, you know. I thought, 'God, what are these fellows we're waiting to meet?' It was unbelievable.

The next thing we saw the bloody flag come down and a Japanese flag go up, so we all had to come out with yer hands up and throw your weapons in. That was a terrible thing and we was surrounded then with Japs, we didn't know there were that many round us but they were coming out of the big monsoon drains, crawling out the drains, they were coming out of houses, they were climbing out of windows, they were all round. You're in the middle of this lot, pointing, you know, bayonets at you.

At the time as a young man I wanted to kind of prove myself by doing something a bit dramatic. But I realized that, you know, it was all a foolish idea, I wasn't the bloody hero you thought you were when the real crunch came. When you saw the Japs with the bayonets there I couldn't tackle one. I knew it. That was me first day as a POW.

They marched us to this Changi village, they kicked all the local people out and wired it all off. It was a very humiliating experience, you know, all throwing yer weapons away and marching along there and it was like a disgrace to us, yet it wasn't our fault.

The first weeks you were just kicked and bashed and punched around. If you didn't move fast enough they were at you with the rifle butts and the boots and God knows what else. They were quick to use the bayonets on people. They were battle-hardened characters and they didn't stand any nonsense.

They told us they'd got this wonderful new project. They were building this marvellous big railway up in Thailand. They said it was a wonderful camp, it was up in a beautiful moderate climate, in the hillside, you'd lovely huts. They gave us all this kind of patter so they said you'll all be happy there and plenty of Red Cross rations.

They packed us all into these trains and it was five days, then we were ten days marching through the jungle. I'd just got the soles left of me shoes, that I managed to tie up. The very next day we were out on the working parties and that was hell on earth. We were shifting great clumps of bamboo, you were digging holes, you were breaking stones, you name it, we were doing it and the Japs were stood over ya all day every hour and every time you stopped they were whacking you with their butts.

It was one continuous mad grind and blokes were just dying every day, you know, somebody was going down with something or other, some were being killed on the site, where they were loosening rocks and it would fall down, and some were falling off bridges that were part built.

I don't know how but you gritted your teeth and made the best of it. I used to do a lot of whatever you could pinch, beg, borrow or steal, we'd eat anything. If you stuck to the rations that the Japs gave you you couldn't survive. We weighed this up very early. Anything that moved, flew or crawled was eaten. We used to try and trap what animals we could. We'd eat iguanas, all these lizards, snakes.

In the early days you used to get really matey with two or three of ya and you'd muck in. You'd build your own little set-up you know and, if yer huts were all leaky and overcrowded, as you went out on a working party you'd bring bits of stuff back with you, bamboo and stuff to patch it up. But you found that the next thing one of them 'ud die suddenly. That's it, it's finished and you'd sat and shared yer bloody memories and yer life with them. You used to be a bit upset, tears flowing in the night, like, so you found it wasn't worth getting close to people. You had to kind of shut it off.

After a few months – I'd had the ordinary dengue fever, dysentery and the general stuff – I got malaria. It was a strange feeling. You're shivering away. You go several weeks pr'haps, free of it, then it's at you again and the more that happens the more damage it does to your system. It affects your spleen and your liver.

It's one of those things that kind of saps your confidence and makes you feel your manhood's at stake. You're degraded, you know, you shouldn't have given in.

Frank spent three years and six months as a prisoner of war. In August 1945 he was in a camp just outside Bangkok, Thailand, building airstrips for the Japanese.

The Japs had been acting strange and they'd kept us all in the day before, brought us all in off the working party which was very

*Frank Davies spent over three years as a POW in the Far East.
The terrible conditions in the camp badly affected Frank's
health — he was on medication for malaria
for many years after the war*

•

unusual. They looked a bit solemn, dejected, and we thought, 'What's happened, has the Emperor died?' I was just going to the well for me rations of water and I saw these strange blokes coming through the camp, and from the distance I thought they looked taller than Japs. Then they were spreading out and the Japs always threatened to kill us all, you see, and so me first instinct was to run. Then I suddenly realized that the big fella there was an English bloke. 'Hello there son, it's all over.' I was nearly fainting and we ended up bloody hugging.

We were a bunch of bloody decrepit skeleton-looking blokes with three and a half years bloody hatred all boiled up. Half of 'em could hardly run, big holes in their legs, bits of cloth with all blood oozing out and all hobbling along. We set the camps on fire, we burnt the lot, they were all bug-ridden huts. And there was tears, there was lots of tears.

There were good blokes that had to take three and a half years to die. There was one or two died on the day we was released. We actually carried some to the aircraft and we put them on this Dakota and the pilot came out, he said, 'You'll have to take these two back off, they've died.'

Eventually they kind of ferried us to this hospital and we all lined up. And we saw a row of the first European women we'd seen in nearly four years and they looked gorgeous, all their white uniforms. They all came out and kind of helped us off the ambulance. There was one on each side of me and I felt that filthy, dirty. I was covered in scabies sores, bits of ulcers on yer legs, ringworm. Your skin went two different colours, you were like brown here and jet-white there and you looked like bloody mottled creatures, you was all skin and bone, beards had grown out of proportion. We were passed through this room and for the first time since we were captured there was this big mirror on the wall and a few of us stopped and, Christ, I looked at meself, you know, I just couldn't believe it. I had to look again to make sure it was me, unbelievable.

When I went in I was fit, A1 and proud of myself. You come home at the age of twenty-four and I'd got all these bloody things wrong with me. I'd got swollen spleen, perforated ear-drum, eyesight needed glasses, teeth had all gone, started to rot, and God knows what. I was having night sweats, nightmares, traumas.

I thought, 'What's the future, what have I done, what have I got to show for my war service?' I felt very inadequate. I was only half-way through the apprenticeship so I had all that to catch up with and finish and it meant going to night school with eighteen-year-olds. You used to take to the drink then, a lot of us did that. Give the grog a bashing to drown your sorrows and that didn't do any good really, it just made it worse. I used to wake up and hadn't a clue where I was. I'd go round feeling the walls. I'd look out the windows to see if there were any Jap guards.

I felt as if I was a coward for not carrying on fighting till I died. I just wanted to bury my head, you know, and pretend it had never happened and the sooner I could get back to work and normality the better. I didn't want to talk about it because to me it was a catastrophe like as if I'd run away from something. I had to bury my pride and say, 'I was a prisoner of war.'

CHAPTER FOUR

The Worker

———— • ————

In the 1930s Ted Clarke was a miner in Scaitcliffe pit near Accrington in Lancashire. He vividly recalls the pride a miner took in his physical strength and endurance. Accidents and injuries would usually be met with a gritty sense of humour, proof that the men were bigger than the dangers they faced.

•

You were classed as a tough guy because it was a tough, really tough, hard job. You'd come out of the pit with scabs on your back from hitting the roof and bark knocked off your knuckles. You were always getting hurt, but you wouldn't show it. Once I hadn't heard these tubs coming and they smashed into me, smashed me leg up. It meant that I'd got to be carried out of the pit, there was no ambulance box or anything like that in those days, all that I got were two little bits of wood strapped to me leg. I were badly shook up. The manager, he saw the accident, I think he was trying to boost me up a bit, he said jokingly, 'tha know Ned, I think this is a bit of a made up do'. I had to have crutches, I was off work thirteen weeks.

•

In the 1900s there were around a million miners, all of them men. This was the archetypal work of the first industrial revolution, dirty and dangerous, hard and exhausting, work that it was assumed only men could do. Even as late as the 1930s coal-cutting machinery was rarely used in many smaller pits and almost half of all coal produced was dug out with pick and shovel, as Joe Crofts remembers.

Before the last war the British economy was dominated by manufacturing industry and around three-quarters of all male workers were manual workers. The vast majority of these men worked in industries that, for the most part, excluded women: mining, iron and steel, heavy engineering, the building industry, the railways, and so on. Most were employed and paid on a weekly basis. In an era when labouring men spent most of their waking hours at work, their work overwhelmingly shaped their lives. It determined to a large extent

Men leaving a dockyard in 1939. Before mass car ownership cycling was a popular way of getting to work.

•

their income, health, home, living standards, friends, private life, and even their leisure. Their work was fundamental to their identity. Although there were a myriad divisions and distinctions amongst workers – notably between skilled and unskilled, and between the 'respectable' and the 'rough' – most thought of themselves as working class. A working-class man, working alongside other men in the pit, in the foundry, in the engine sheds, had a distinct identity and inhabited a quite different daytime world from that of most women or from men in other classes of society.

One of the great citadels of male working-class power and privilege was the labour aristocracy – craftsmen, engineers, boilermakers – skilled workmen who had served their time and who jealously guarded their superior status and earnings. At the pinnacle of this hierarchy, in prestige if not in wages, was the engine driver. To drive a steam engine was the dream of most schoolboys. Amongst the engine drivers there was immense pride in work, especially in punctuality, to bring a train in exactly on time. And perhaps more than in any other industry there was an extraordinarily close relationship between man and machine. Many firemen and drivers regarded their locomotives as almost human – it was an art to know how to treat them and get the best out of them. Dave Bowman, an engine driver in the 1940s, remembers the strong attraction of the speed and power of the old steam locomotives.

The men employed by the railway companies, each with their own splendid livery, formed part of a new breed of uniformed worker – policemen, firemen, postmen, and so on – who had been swelling the ranks of the working class from Victorian times onwards. Governed by an ethic of public duty and service these workers were subject to a host of bureaucratic rules and regulations and military-style discipline. In the police force and the fire brigade – jobs that involved risking life to protect members of the public – masculine values of strength, courage and heroism were immensely important. New police recruits quickly learned they had to be tough and not display emotion in order to do the job. Glyn Davies was a young policeman in Sheffield in the 1940s:

•

It was the first time I'd seen a person who'd committed suicide and it was a dreadful sight. And I went downstairs and let the inspector and the other policeman in and I'm afraid I felt rather emotional about this. 'What's happened?' They said, 'pull yourself together lad.' It was the same if you were called to a nasty road accident, you couldn't start crying or gnashing your teeth there. There was a job to be done wasn't there, you've no time to cry and you mustn't. Well, what if you saw a policeman crying, you'd think he was mad wouldn't you?'

•

Suppression of emotion together with a rigid division of labour between men and women was also characteristic of the work culture of the fishing industry in which around 100 000 worked during the inter-war years. Although women played an important role on the quayside, gutting, smoking and packing the fish, it was only men who went to sea. (Amongst the many superstitions of fishermen was the belief that a woman who set foot on a boat would bring the crew ill fortune). The men on the herring fleets and deep-sea trawlers went off for weeks at a time. Their work in the stormy and unpredictable North Sea was arduous and dangerous. In fact, fishing was the most dangerous occupation of all – during the Edwardian era as many as 500 fishermen were lost every year. This was a rugged male culture where, despite the risk to life, it was taboo to admit fear, as Geordie Todd, a North Shields trawler skipper in the 1930s recalls.

*In stormy weather, waves in the North Sea could often reach up to thirty feet
in height. Even in dangerous conditions it was taboo
for fisherman to show fear.*

•

At home fisherman were unusual in their willingness to help cook and clean – skills they learned at sea where there were no women to look after them. But most men, especially men who did heavy labouring jobs, generally refused to do any domestic chores. This was not seen as man's work and was threatening to his masculinity. It was widely assumed that a woman's place was in the home and married women found it very difficult to find paid employment. In the 1930s, 95 per cent of married women with children did not work outside the home. For most men it was a matter of pride and status that their wife did not go out to work. The division of labour was simple: the man was the breadwinner and the woman was the home-maker. David Swift, a labourer on building-sites in Nottingham in the 1950s, remembers how ingrained these attitudes used to be: 'Your job was to go to work and bring home money to keep them and provide them with warmth and clothing. I was told that was my job. And when I came home and my dinner wasn't ready, piping hot on the table, there was trouble, there was arguments, because I anticipated that was how life was.'

If a man could not provide for his family he was thought a failure. Mass unemployment during the inter-war years – rising to over three million in the early 1930s – consequently proved to be a crushing blow for male pride, especially as unemployment was concentrated in old industries like mining where masculinity was so highly prized. George Short, an unemployed miner in County Durham in the 1930s remembers: 'The main feeling was not so much of anger but of frustration. The average man, particularly the men of my class, they always believed that they were the breadwinner and the fact that the wife got a job didn't help, because that helped to take away from the man the sense of importance which was his. I saw people become completely demoralized and their sense of manliness began to deteriorate just because they had not got a job and because they weren't able to provide the things that they believed their family was entitled to.'

To find work, many unemployed men entered new occupations and left their home communities. Some joined the Army – customarily the last resort of the unemployed in peacetime – and during the 1930s there was an increase in recruitment from depressed areas like Scotland and South Wales. Tom Hopkins was one of the new recruits from the valleys, but unable to stomach army discipline he deserted

A Derbyshire miner and his family in the early 1900s.
Providing for a wife and children could be a constant struggle
for the working-class father.

•

and used his skills as a fighter to make a living as a fairground booth boxer.

Mining and manufacturing industry, and the old kind of manual labour that went with it, was in general decline during the first half of the century. Employment in the coal industry, for example, fell by almost half a million, from 1 200 000 in 1911 to 700 000 in 1938. But the number employed in offices, doing less physically demanding work in a clean and comfortable environment, was becoming more important as the service sector of the economy expanded. Jobs in offices had traditionally been viewed as unmanly by manual workers – the pen-pushing clerk with his suit and tie, rolled umbrella and superior airs and graces, had long been a figure of fun and resentment amongst working-class men. The idea that 'real men' didn't work in offices was reinforced by the new trend towards recruiting single women into clerical jobs. However, the growth in clerical and lower grade professional work in offices forced more and more men to question their assumptions about the effeminacy of office work.

Frank Davies recalls how switching from a shop floor to an office job for Metro-Vickers in the 1940s involved a change of identity:

•

I felt a bit embarrassed when you'd go back in the workshops and you had to go into the same departments where you worked. I used to creep past me old mates with me suit on. I felt they were looking at me as if I wasn't doing man's work any more, taken over a girl's job in other words, they looked upon that as a thing that women should be doing, not grown men. I used to feel a bit like this. I thought, here's me with me papers under me arm, me best suit on and they're up to their eyes in muck and banging away at the job and there were all the wisecracks about the job I'd taken. But gradually I think it dawned on a lot of them that there was more to life than that. I used to explain to some of them, I said 'You know me, I've worked as hard as any of you lot and I know now which is the hardest mentally.' I says, 'I go home more tired than you ever did, you go home and forget it, I can't, I got to get certain things ready for morning to go in and see me manager'. So you know, we got through it.

•

The mass recruitment of women, during the two world wars, into jobs traditionally done by men also began to break the mould of rigid ideas about men and women's work. With men away fighting at the Front, millions of women proved that they could do most manual labour jobs as well as men could. Nelson Fowler, a farmer in North Devon, remembers how the presence of the Women's Land Army during the Second World War began to change attitudes towards women as workers. But deep down – probably like most farmers of his generation – he felt that a woman's proper place was in the home.

Ideas about what was proper work for men and women remained deeply entrenched. In 1945 women were told to leave their jobs to make way for the returning men, much as they had after the First World War. And in the professions the prejudice against women was almost as strong as it was on the shop floor. There was a long-standing and widely imposed bar on the employment of married women in many professions like education and the Civil Service. Even when these formal barriers began to be dismantled during and after the last war there remained an immensely strong bias towards the recruitment and promotion of men. Men, it was assumed, were most endowed with the qualities, like rational thought and competitiveness, that were essential for success. And there was the 'old boys' network' which was deeply suspicious towards the entry of women. One of the last bastions of male professional domination was the City of London and its financial institutions. Dundas Hamilton remembers how, as late as the 1950s, there was a strong desire to keep the Stock Exchange for men only and how women were seen as best suited to secretarial work.

A member of the Stock Exchange photographed in 1951. The bowler hat and black suit were part of the strict dress code for working in the City.

The Stock Exchange was finally opened to women in 1973, part of a new wave of pressure for equal rights and opportunities for women in the workplace. The impact of this movement however had been limited, not least because of the surprising resilience of pre-war male attitudes towards work of the sort recalled in the stories that follow. At the heart of this traditional view of the division of labour between men and women is the notion that the natural role of the male is to be a breadwinner and that the most physically and mentally demanding jobs are best done by men.

Nelson Fowler

•

Nelson lives in Newton St Petrock, a tiny village close to Bideford, Devon. His bungalow is about a quarter of a mile away from the farm which has been in his family since Victorian times. Nelson had just celebrated his ninety-first birthday when we filmed him, but he is still a very active man. His face reflects a lifetime spent out in all weathers. Red-cheeked, with a broad North Devon accent, he looks every inch the country farmer. As the only boy, with three sisters, Nelson took over the farm from his father in 1939. It is now in the hands of Nelson's eldest son George, and his wife Shirley. His grandson Andrew works on the farm, too, and will take over when the time comes.

•

I wouldn't like to lose the name I don't think, the Fowler name. I mean there's a lot of Joneses and Thomases and names like that more, but you wouldn't find a Fowler farming anywhere around for a dozen parishes. Being the only boy, Father would say, 'The farm's yours after me. Can't carry on without you.'

I can remember as a little boy, father lifting me up on the horse and he'd walk along and catch me by the leg, hold me leg so I wouldn't fall off. I weren't no more than four or five year old I don't think then and I've been riding horses all me life.

I never liked school very much. I was working half the time and they'd keep you home, you know. When you'd got a lot of work to do you could stay home from school for a few days.

First thing when I come down of a morning was go to the stable, feed the horses before I had me breakfast, then clean the stable out. Then mother'd be shouting breakfast was ready or something. The horses would be feeding all the time I'd had my breakfast and had cleaned up. Come down and give 'em a light brushing over, you'd be ready to go out in the fields and work with them.

My father was gifted. He used to do a lot of ploughing in them days. He taught me the way to plough and fix a plough well. There's an art to it, very much an art.

Some people prided theirselves in it more than others. Some would go out and plough crooked. But honestly as you start and after I'd been a few runs I would have a straight furrow and I never

Above: *Before the mecha-
nization of farming, working
the land with horses meant
long hours of exhausting
work. Despite this, farmers
often enjoyed
a close relationship with
their animals.*

•

*Nelson Fowler on his farm in Newton St Petrock,
Devon, with two of his prized shire horses.*

•

ploughed crooked in my life hardly. I'd plough as straight as a line, you know. I'd got that sort of gift and sort of prided meself in that a bit. Somebody would say, 'Old Farmer Fowler's son over there he's a good ploughman int'e?'

I was getting on a bit when I took over. I was twenty-eight before I was married, you see. I stayed along of my father and helped look after the place pretty well. I felt it a bit when he went and I had got it all. It was a bit of a shock but I wasn't worried much because I used to help manage nearly everything in the last.

I got three sisters and well they all married and went away but you know we were sort of a family farm, it was more or less the family together. Well, it seemed to me that women got a lot to do in the farmhouses and they used to make the butter, pounds of butter. Then going to market and sell twenty pounds of butter.

They weren't quite like the men, you see, they weren't going to make their lives at farming with horses, whereas the boys and that was coming bigger and better all the time and they'd get men and be able to do the farm work. The girls, well, they got married or something and they didn't carry on, but it wasn't quite like the men, I don't think, not the girls.

I've never been out and that I couldn't catch a horse. I know once, I had a work chap there, and my horses had broke in a neighbour's there and I said, 'You bring 'em back Charlie'. Well he couldn't catch 'em. So I said, 'Charlie, if I go down there and if I can't come home with the horse I'll give 'e the 'orse.' I brought the horse back all right, you know, it's a bit of gift that. I used to treat horses right. You have a pocket of oats and when you let the horse go or when you take the halter off, give 'im a mouthful of oats, well he'd remember that next time, you see, and he'd come up.

When the war started we got the Land Army women. There's one thing I'll praise them for, they were wonderful patriotic. They wasn't out fighting but they helped out with everything they could at 'ome.

We used to put in a lot of time with the horses on our farm, I know we did, to be a good horseman. The Land Girls liked the horses but didn't always have the right way with them. Some girl that we got was bringing one horse and cart back and I was bringing the other. Well, she come over and opened the gate and went through and let the horse go instead of holding on to 'un. I come through and I was coming up when her horse moved away. Everything in this cart went flying and the horse galloped down the field and across the stream at the bottom and got hung up in the gate. Well, this girl, if she'd been a man he would have held the horse you see, but the girl wasn't quite capable. We preferred the men, I think we did. Lifting sacks and things like that, the women wasn't quite as strong. They was willing but they wasn't really up to handling a farm horse.

We all liked the son to carry on some farming, you see, we all did. Learning's a wonderful thing, but going on to school until you'm eighteen or twenty and then go farming, it isn't quite so good as it is if you take on about twelve or fourteen. You sort of come right up with it, you see. I rather think that's the best way.

Even George, my son, he won the Young Farmers' Ploughing Match there, George did. Well, I told 'un how to plough a bit I know, and then George he ploughed in the Open and he was third in the Open I think, that very year. I wanted the name to stay, as a Fowler, and I thought perhaps he'd be a farmer. Well, George is a farmer now.

Geordie Todd

•

He did not follow his father down the pit, but started inshore fishing as a fourteen-year-old in 1926. In 1928 he began on the trawlers, and rose to become a skipper in three years. His first ship was the John Donovan. *He remained a skipper until he retired in 1977. He still loves the sea, and the fishing life. He goes to the Seaman's Mission twice a week for his fish lunch, and he spends a lot of time at the quayside talking to the men as they work. During the filming we took him out on a trawler – it was the first time he had been to sea in seventeen years – and he loved it.*

•

I saw me old skipper and I was telling him I was taking the *John Donovan* away. He says, 'When you become skipper, and you get a boat of your own, you got to prove that you are skipper and take no notice of anybody. You're in charge of that boat and you got to make her pay and make sure your authority stands.'

Well this trip I came aboard expecting just to step aboard and be

Geordie Todd aged nineteen in 1931 on his first voyage as a skipper.

•

off. Well, bunker lids wasn't on, no coal, still the coal was on the deck. I asked the mate where the fireman was. He was lying on the settee. So I went to him and he was lying there, he'd had a few drinks like. So I just picked him up like that, banged him against the side of the cabin. He went straightaway and put the lids on and of course when we did the trip and come the end again I sacked him and I got another fireman. After that we went smashing, no problem at all.

When you're in command of a boat you've got to show your authority, and to show it you've got to live up to what you say. Whatever you say you've got to carry it out, sometimes it doesn't always turn out to be as it should be but once you've made the decision – no turning back.

I used to say if any of the crew want any special fish they should come and ask me. If he steals it he gets the sack, simple as that. They'd start to respect ya and they would talk among theirselves and say, 'Oh if you do that, if you pinch that, you've had it, the skipper'll sack ya.'

'Course when you have a crew like that and they start to respect you it goes a long way. When you land on the market the next morning and one of the crew comes to you and says, 'Skipper can I have a bit fish,' I told them to take it, help yourself and that's the way it should be. I had a lot of respect from my crew.

I just wanted to get them to accept the discipline that I made for my boat and that rubbed off on to them from one hand to the next one. A new hand stepped aboard the boat he knew exactly what to expect. I was a hard worker and I expected everybody under us to work as hard as me.

I used to go guttin' and mend the net, a lot of skippers wouldn't, they would tell their mate what to do. Not me, I used to go down and get me hand in and I used to train the deck hands all about the net, the way I was taught. There was no half washing of the fish, just quick swill. All the blood had to be off, otherwise the fish didn't keep. Nobody had to skive.

You must work together, pull together. It is really all for one and one for all, sort of style. If you didn't then you had trouble. Somebody would go over the side.

Everybody's delighted when they see a floating bag of fish. It's all coppers in the pocket then. If you've got a good haul it'll show a really boiling blob away from the boat side, a white boiling blob and that's the air coming out the fish. That's another successful haul but if there's no white mark, no boil then you know that you got nothing.

As long as there was fish on the deck I could keep me crew on the deck. Whether it was thirty hours, forty hours, fifty hours, didn't make any difference. I could keep me crew on the deck till they dropped and many a time I've seen decks full, couldn't shoot the net for more, we had to wait while we got one side in the clear.

If you had a deck full of fish speed is essential to get all that last haul down below before the next one came. You'd see the knives going like that, yes, a good crowd could clear a lot of fish away in an hour.

When you're gutting the cod you just grab the cod by the head, stuck your knife in his belly, slit it open, put your hand in and pulled his guts out and then it was off. Cod was thrown over one side ready to be washed. Maybe five seconds, ten seconds, that's all it took unless it was roe season and then you had to take the roe out the cod very delicately. You didn't want to bust that, 'cos that was your pocket money.

You never felt tired as long as you saw fish coming aboard and of course the cook was always on the go with plenty of tea, tons of tea, great big pint mugs. After you got a couple of them down you you were as right as rain for another ten hours. But as soon as you touched yer bunk you were asleep. I've seen them fall asleep with a cigarette in their finger and burn their fingers they were that exhausted.

It's a great reward for your labours and when you go in the office on settling day and you get a packet and there's money in that packet and your wife's been drawing her allotment every Friday and you got money in your pocket, you're king of the castle then, aye.

A lot of fishermen are superstitious and if you have a superstitious skipper of course he's in command, he wields the glove. You never scrub the deck, all the blood's left on the deck till it's washed off by water coming aboard. If you use a deck brush the skipper, oh, he used to go mad. 'Shift that bloody brush off there.' People used to say you shouldn't sail on a Friday as well, it brought the ship bad luck but I wasn't superstitious at all until I had the first accident.

I sailed, Friday, I think three days or four days and the mate collapsed and died of a heart attack. I just had to haul the trawl and proceed back to port with the body. So the next day I sailed again and the deck hand come to us in the wheel house, held his hand up and his three fingers and a thumb was hanging to a hair. I took him down and got a bag of flour and put his hand in to stop the bleeding and proceeded back to port. Next morning I was just going to go out the door and I went in to see the wife. She says, 'Well, be careful George, trouble comes in threes.' I thought that was bloody old woman's tale and I'm walking down the lighthouse stairs and a chap come up. 'Skipper of the *John Donovan*? 'Well, you'll not get away the day. She just blew the bottom door off the boiler.'

Well, then I did believe in the three troubles and if I got one trouble I used to say, 'Please God, don't let anything else happen.'

In the winter time in the North Sea – January, February was the two worst months – that's when you got the snow and the frost, and if you were working close inland it was always colder. We never shaved at sea and I've seen the frost on your beard and if you went to rub it your beard would break 'cos it was always frozen.

When you're fishing, the boat has a gentle roll, even in bad weather, just slowly. You're not driving her hard and therefore she just rides up on the top and over the next, down the next one, then up over the top. But if you're steaming, no gear, no trawl over the side, then's the trouble. You take the heavy water and then you're in trouble sometimes. You smash yer gear up, smash yer wheel up and the likes of that when you take heavy sea. But a fisherman never feels any hazard in bad weather, you just think to yourself, 'It's here, we've got to get on with it.' When you're in bad weather like that you think of the lost revenue, that's the main thing you think of – pounds, shilling and pence. The skipper hadn't to show any fear, he had to be always saying, 'Nothing to worry about.'

A wave in the North Sea would reach anything from twenty to thirty feet, sometimes more. Night time was the most scary part, everything's black dark and you see a crest of sea rolling up towards you and you wonder whether it's going to go underneath or over the top of you, and that's when all the damage is done. She'll smash the wheel house, she'll smash everything when you get a lump of water maybe ten, fifteen, twenty ton dropping on your deck. It makes yer boat shudder at times. It's deafening when it's pounding on the deck and you hear the wind howling through the rigging, 'cos mind it does whistle.

Might have a felt a little bit rumble in the tummy but you would never show it. Especially as a skipper you had to take it. If a fisherman can't stand a bit of storm weather then he's no good. If you showed fear you weren't a man.

If you've been in really bad weather and you come back home and you're bringing your boat in through the piers safely, you think it's great. You're really pleased with yourself when you come ashore and the old skippers is standing on the bank top watching you.

Dave Bowman

•

Dave is extremely confident, fit and lively. He is an animated and powerful speaker, especially when talking about trains. Born in Dundee in 1913, he joined the London and North Eastern Railway Company as a cleaner in 1930, and worked his way up to driver in 1949. Always involved in the railways trade union movement he became President of the NUR in 1970, a post he held for three years. His story-telling is passionate, and it takes the listener over. His stories are experiences relived, with sound effects and movements. He has a room at his home in Brighton dedicated to trains, with plaques on the wall, pictures, and all manner of railway memorabilia.

•

It was a great feeling of independence, being in charge of possibly the most powerful machine on land. After all you were driving a machine that was three hundred and eighty tons with possibly four hundred tons of beef or fish or maybe eight hundred passengers sitting in it. I used to love Sunday school picnics and you saw all the kids coming down piling into the train and taking them away for a

Sunday afternoon picnic. All these little kids, they thought it was wonderful, particularly when they went over the Tay bridge and all the kids were at the window pointing to the old bridge. I was the person who was in charge of the train that was taking them, I had the responsibility, I was the boy.

I loved the whole railway life and I treated everyone on the railway as I hoped they would treat me – as an equal. We were all in a happy family. We had a football team, boxing teams, we'd all kinds of things going on. It was all a community, everyone working together, and I loved that.

I started off cleaning the engines. We had three shifts, day shift, what we called back shift, starting at two o'clock, and a night shift starting at ten p.m. and you went around the rota. There would be about sixteen cleaners on each shift.

It was a masculine job. I remember cleaning the wheels of one of these big Pacific engines. There was a little white rim around the green, the London North-eastern Green, and you had to clean it all perfect because if a driver came out he'd say, 'Listen son, you've left a bit grease on here.' So it had to be absolutely perfect.

The sheds were all male until during the war, some women came on during the war, they were a bloody nuisance. You couldn't get a woman to stand in a pit holding up a big end on her shoulder, it just wasn't possible. But they never came on the footplate, they got on as guards and did some good jobs as guards.

In steam days there was a great camaraderie among all railwaymen. I'm in the NUR, we're all together, we're all railwaymen. You had the guard, the fireman and the driver and that was the train team. We used to have some good fun. When you'd twenty minutes for your break, you used to have races. If you were in the Celtic pit you would challenge the miners to a hundred yards race, something like that.

If you saw a football match in the early morning, six o'clock when we all come off the shift, between eleven LMS men and eleven LNER men playing for six pence a side, you would know it. They'd play their heart out. 'These swines from the LNER.' 'These bastards from the LMS.' It was good competition, never any serious intent. You had to play, because if you let the side down you were in trouble.

But I must say that everyone always wanted to get away from the cleaning on to the firing and on to the driving. You advanced

Dave Bowman was a driver with the LNER in the 1940s.
Oiling a steam locomotive was a major task which had to be carried out by the driver
before leaving the engine shed.

•

through the cleaner, never jumping over anyone, through seniority until you become the top cleaner and then you went on as the first vacancy for a fireman, until you became the top fireman and then you became the junior driver.

As an engine driver you were top of your job, you couldn't get any higher, so there you are. I didn't expect anyone to say, 'Isn't he a wonderful fellow?' It was respect for myself, an inner self-respect. 'Yes, mate, you're done it and you've got there.' That's fine.

To be moving every day, not to be sitting on your arse in an office, not to be serving in a shop and saying, 'Madam.' To be out and doing something and moving with this power of the locomotive. It was a great romance, and all young men were attracted to it. The fellow who could be a good engine driver and could hold his own, as I could, with all around, you were very proud to be an engine driver.

I loved the power of the engine. Coming out of Aberdeen you'd open the throttle, you were away and you were in charge, independence. You were the guy who was doing it. Looking at these big side rods there would be a little steam issuing and it would go 'Shh, shh, shh.' And I used to think 'Yeah, that's power, power'. You felt all this weight coming behind you and going wonderful, 'Sshh, shh'. You could feel the engine juddering and then when you got speed up to the top of the bank you're up to about eighty-five, ninety, ninety-five miles an hour. 'Whish.' And then passing the North Sea, sometimes the sea coming in with the wind coming in with the sea, and the big waves coming up and you're flashing past at eighty-five, wonderful.

When you're going through a tunnel you're met with this black wall. Now you know at the other end you get out because you've done it yesterday or the day before, you're not running into a brick wall. The important thing is to make sure you get the blower in so that the fire doesn't come back into the firebox and burn the fireman first and then you. So you go into this tunnel and there's a roar and there's a sulphur smell because the smoke box ashes are hitting the roof of the tunnel. So you keep your head in, you don't have your head out the cab because sulphur ashes are coming down on to your face. Now that's it, you come out the tunnel, put the blower off and on you go.

Everyone drove their own way. I always brought it down to fifteen slightly and then release it again so that the train came to a stand. I always said you could put a little Scotch threepenny bit at the end of the platform and I could stop on that or I wouldn't be far off it.

The thing was to stop the bloody thing at the right place, where the passengers wanted to get out on the platform, and also to run the train without spilling all the people's coffee that are in the back.

Speed was very important but more important was punctuality. I remember there was one train we run to Glasgow and you went down a hill in a tunnel and then you came out in the station and there was a huge clock at the end of the station with a second hand. The fireman saw the clock before I did, and I would say to the fireman, 'Look to see if we're on time.' He would turn round to me and say, 'You're nineteen seconds late.'

Driving at night was easier than driving during the day, because you saw the signals better and you run the train by the signals. One of the things I loved about night driving was in certain parts of the autumn there up in the night sky as you came up north you would see these huge lights – red, green, purple all swinging around. Just a huge array of lights and I used to say to the fireman, 'Come here, d'you see that? That's the aurora borealis and you are a very privileged person to be able to look at that because there are millions of people that can't look because they're lying in their bloody bed and don't know it's there.'

Tom Hopkins

•

You would not miss Tom Hopkins in a crowd. His shock of bright white hair marks him out, so too does the placard he carries with him daily in Caerphilly town centre. He makes his regular pilgrimage to stand outside the local supermarket, with a placard spreading the socialist gospel. He has been politically active since his youth. Now eighty-four, he is a well-known local character. Tom joined the Army in 1929, after four years of working as a miner. He was arrested for fighting when he was twenty-two, and spent six months in a military jail before he was dismissed. He then spent two years working as a stoker on ships. In 1935 he left the ship in Dundee, and travelled round Scotland in search of work.

•

Tom Hopkins photographed in his early twenties. He grew up in a mining family in Caerphilly with six brothers and seven sisters.

•

I used to go down the gym every day and learn boxing. And I used to do a lot of fighting in the streets, sparring. Not to hit anybody hard or anything like that but everybody used to come out on their doorstep and watch us you know, and they enjoyed it.

Then one day there was a big fair in Glasgow so I went there and had a look around and there was a boxing booth. There was going to be a boxing match that night so I asked the fellow and he said, 'Aye, do you want to volunteer to fight?'

That's how I got started. That night I went there and they come out on the platform and the boss of the gym says, 'Will anybody stand four rounds with so-and-so and they'll get two pounds?' So I said I would. He was about the same weight as me and I went in and in the second round I knocked him out. They had the shock of their lives, every bugger was shouting and bawling, hooraying and God knows what.

So anyway the boss said to me, 'Would you like to join the gym? We got a caravan for you to sleep and you get your meals, and a couple of quid a week for boxing.' You had to take on all comers. And he said he thought I could do that. So I said, I'd have a go. It was a lot of money and I fancied the life it would mean, travelling round with the fair.

I used to train like hell in there like and we used to go from Dundee to Lanark and all over the place. I attracted a lot of people into the boxing booth, and so they were very pleased with that and he kept me on longer.

Two or three days in a week our job was then to help in the stalls around the place, if you had a day off you'd try and train like 'ell. They made sure that it was boxing on a Saturday because that's when all the crowds come, on a Saturday, and it would be advertised for

Hughes Boxing Pavilion in the mid 1930s. Mass unemployment forced many young men to fight for a living in these travelling boxing booths.

•

that effect and of course the main thing is that the boxers belonging to the gym would stand on the stage in their boxing kit all ready and if anybody in the crowd fancied they're going to win a couple of quid, well they'd have a go. The crowd always used to give a good cheer when somebody volunteered and somebody always volunteered 'cos two quid in those days was a lot of money. So they weren't backward in coming forward and all they wanted then was hoping that the booth boxer would be beaten.

If you're going to box you've trained like hell to be able to – or that particular night that you're going to box and if you weaken yourself in any way by having sexual intercourse the night before, two days before if you like, it affects your punching power. If you get punched like 'ell after having sex and you're weakened it's no good. so I used to concentrate my mind solely on boxing.

I used to sit down before the fight and think of what my programme would be, what I would do. 'Now the first round I'll just go round and see what he's like, keep away and all the rest of it, but the second round now I'm going to smash in one punch, if I can.' My mind was always set on what I'm going to do so it never gave you a chance to feel frightened because if you felt frightened you might as well finish. You're defeated before you go in, so you go in there with the determination that you were going to win and if you lose, well you lose, if you get hurt well you get hurt and you take it that way. But the point is this, if you are trained properly and looked after yourself properly you know that you can protect yourself by ducking and diving.

Sometimes he'll shoot out with his left and you'll knock it apart like that, knock it over and then you'd bang as 'ard as you can and if you could get him on the chin you know he's knocked out and that's how I used to do it.

The crowd watching the boxing matches were always full of praise or you'd get them all moaning and groaning if you had a miss. They'd be shouting and bawling but if you was successful and you was giving the other fellow a bit of a hammering well then they would be shouting, 'Hooray, good boy.' You couldn't hear when you was boxing really, all you was worried about was the fellow in front of you. Your mind is fully occupied in trying to think how you're going to beat your opponent.

Every time that the opponent knocked the booth boxer and give him a good punch it was a roar then, the crowd would hooray and everything else and say carry on and hit him out and all this. As far as the booth boxer was concerned he's supposed to be great but sometimes they'd get knocked out too, and the crowd would then go haywire, you might have a fellow that wasn't all that great as a boxer but he'd put everything into one punch and caught the fellow, 'cos you can't always avoid that punch, like, you know. If you lose once or twice well that's all right but if you're losing all the time they don't want you because they know that you're not capable of being in the booth, so they couldn't put up you against anybody and so they'd sack you.

The great thing is, of course, that you keep yourself fit. You got a chance in life then if you're fit and your body can take all sorts of punishment. It makes you feel good and strong and confident. 'I'm a boxing champion and that's great.'

Joe Crofts

•

Joe worked at Brookhouse Colliery in Beighton, near Sheffield from 1927 until 1960. He remembers, with a mixture of fondness and resignation, the daily grind of a miner's lot in the thirties. The work was arduous and, after thirty-three years at the pit, Joe was determined to try a different kind of work above ground. He and his wife Marie moved to Preston and Joe found work as a bus driver. He retired in 1988.

•

It was man's work, on the coal face. A coal miner didn't go home tired, he went, with the pick and the shovel, he went home exhausted. I can remember times when I'd seen my stint out, but I hadn't really recovered next day. You're still aching from the day before although you've been to bed.

Pick and shovel work in the old days was what it says, it was pick and shovel. You'd top chop your coal out, shovel it and they used to have a bar, we called 'em ringers. With that and your pick and your shovel, you got your coal, and it was 'ard work. I used to have segs here on my hand like a piece of leather. You never blistered because yer hands adapted to a point where they were like leather.

You had to grasp your pick and you couldn't hold a pick with gloves on, it would slip. So you had to spit on yer hands. Anybody to have worn gloves they'd have said, 'Get them gloves off, what you doing? Get them gloves off like.' I think it was to do with the fact that you can't do that job right with them on, it was that attitude. 'Tha can't do it reet like that.' If tha knows what I mean.

There was some powerful men that could do it because they had the muscle, they had the brawn and they had the stamina. They was always the top machos, top men at work, filling the most yardage. They were strong men, powerful men. The more yards you took the more money you got and they'd more money to spend. So they used invariably to be the macho drinkers. They were trying to prove themselves manly. It was part of being the man you know, the big man and they were held in a bit of esteem. It was respect, part fear. You wouldn't have gone to one of these blokes and out and out insulted him like while he were in drink.

A Derbyshire miner working with a pick and shovel in 1910. Over a million men were employed in the coal industry in Edwardian Britain.

•

But there were some colliers that were just average men so to speak. I were never a powerful bloke, but I was fit and if you were fit that was one of the big factors. You had to be from the sweating and filling, well, average about sixteen tons per day out.

I've worked in seams that were only three foot six high. It wasn't high enough to lift yer drinking bottle up to drink out on it, it was that low, like.

It was real exhaustion when you got 'ome like. You went 'ome and you went to sleep in your pit dirt. You could cough up coal at end of day, you're coughing up stuff black as looking at a piece of coal. You just slumped down and you were out. I've gone 'ome on lates, sometime, I've got home about half-past eleven in my pit dirt, had a bit of supper and dropped asleep in chair. Next thing it's two o'clock in the morning and I'm still not bathed.

Some days you went to work you hadn't recovered from the day before, your body ached. You hadn't got your sweat back. You didn't feel like walking the three miles to pit but once you got going and working you were back in the swing again.

I used to get home at twelve o'clock in morning and the wife used to have me a plate of chips and steak and I could hardly see over top of pile of chips. We were working so hard, our physical work was so great that we worked it off.

You feel terrible some days. You thought, 'God, how am I going to do it today?' The roof would be bad and you'd to spend half your time propping up, time when you should be shovelling coal so you're far behind with your break. At end of day if you'd a lot of coal left and hadn't the time to move it they used to have to send men down to 'elp ya and they didn't like doing that.

Bad roof was the reason why it wasn't always easy and sometimes the coal were down, what we used to call it. You steadily learnt how to put up the supports and all the little bits and bats that goes to making experienced collier. How to test a roof with your pick to see whether it's safe and how to tell when coal's breaking. The coals are on the bottoms, that means the weight had come down on 'em and pinned 'em and you had to get to the back of the cut. You literally had to chop your way into back of cut. They used to fire shots into it and it used to make hardly any difference.

I got me jaw broken, I got me foot broke twice, across me foot and I had me leg broke just below knee. The worst accident was behind a power loader, this was later, when the power loaders came in. You had to set your supports, two uprights and a steel bar across top and it was my job to hand the steel bar over to the man that was actually setting it. I was leaned over the back end of the bar, the steel bar and a big rock fell out on the other end of the bar and it was like a lever and it lifted that end up and my jaw, was right over it. Took me up into roof and smashed all me jaw, and well that was how it were.

I didn't lose consciousness but I were in like a half-sense if you will. I could see people and it's one of them conditions where you know what's going on and yet it's a hazy kind of thing. The charge hand behind said, 'Well, d'you think you can walk Joe?' I said, 'Aye I can walk, he's hurting bad but I can walk.' And I walked the three miles to pit bottom.

We got to the shaft bottom and the man in charge said, 'No, while we're winding coal up and down the shaft we can't stop, only for special reasons.'

So the charge hand said, 'Well, let this chap out like, he's got a broken jaw.'

He said, 'Well, he don't look to have a broken jaw to me.' That were with me walking, you see.

So I says, 'Aye, I'm getting a broken jaw all right.' Best way I could like. I'm not making meself out some kind of a strong man but I did walk that distance. I was a bit dazy but I were prepared to walk sooner than somebody carry me all that way, and that's how it were.

Dundas Hamilton

•

He was educated at Rugby and Cambridge. Extremely eloquent and fluent, he speaks with great confidence. At the beginning of the Second World War Dundas joined the Artillery and was demobbed a lieutenant-colonel – at twenty-six , the youngest in the British Army. After the war he stood as a Conservative MP. In 1946 he joined his father's stockbroking firm in the City, and is still a well-respected man in his field. He lives in Central London, but spends weekends with his wife in the country.

•

I had two alternatives, one was to go into my father's firm in the Stock Exchange or to go back to university and became a research chemist. Well, by that time, I'd had seven years in the Army and I thought I'd like to earn some money for myself, so I joined his firm.

I was not alone, of course, in joining my father's firm. There was a very large number of people who went into the family business, and nepotism, if you like, or family relations were very strong in those days. In fact one of the strengths of the Stock Exchange and one of the reasons that you trusted people was your father trusted their fathers and you trusted the sons so the relationship was very close.

The first job that you got in the Stock Exchange, if you were destined to be probably a partner or to go into the higher echelons, at that time was to be a 'blue button'. A 'blue button' was an unauthorized dealer. In your lapel you wore a little blue and white button – a

Dundas Hamilton worked as a partner in a firm of stock brokers in the City during the 1940s and 50s.

•

big blue circle in the middle with a little white circle round it and that was the name 'blue button'. When you went up to a jobber, who was the market maker in the shares, he knew immediately that you could not do a transaction. You could ask a price, you could give a message, you could run an errand, but he couldn't deal with you because you were a 'blue button.' That was the job that you did for a two-year apprenticeship before you were eligible to become a member.

Well, the City was very much a male-orientated place. For a start, you could not become a member of the Stock Exchange unless you were male. Most of the members, and certainly most of the partners in firms, were public school, so all the ethics and all the codes of behaviour of the public school came down to the Stock Exchange.

One of the reasons, I think, that we didn't welcome women was because we weren't used to them. There were no women at public schools. We hadn't been brought up with women of the same age as ourselves and I think, on the whole, men trusted each other. They knew they could speak frankly to each other – there were no holds barred. Trust is the main quality that is required in the City of London.

I remember we had a referendum amongst Stock Exchange members as to whether we should change the rules and admit women, and I voted strongly against it. I could see no reason at all to spoil what was really a very satisfactory situation by admitting women. In our office women could do two things. They could either be secretaries or they could be comptometer [calculator] operators. The idea that they could become a partner, or even become a research assistant, was something that we didn't even contemplate.

There was a much greater degree of formality between the sexes I think, then, than there is now. For example, there were no Christian name terms. I didn't call my secretary by her Christian name, I called her Miss Barker. She called me Mr Hamilton and if I wanted to ask her a question I would phone across and ask her to come and see me and settle her down and then ask her a question and then she would go back again. I didn't even ask her questions on the telephone. She came to see me to get the question and answer it. You treated the ladies in the firm as ladies, because that's what they were. There was no question of them being equal with you, or inferior to you, they were a different lot of people and you treated them like that.

You will know that the motto of the Stock Exchange is 'My word is my bond'. That means that if I make a mistake I bear the consequences, so if I were to have an order, for example, to sell five thousand shares and by mistake I buy five thousand shares, then I've got to go and put it right at my own expense. Though one trusted women socially, and I trusted women of course, maritally, trusting them with a million pounds' worth of business or trusting them with exactly complying with the nuances of dealing, was not something that one would actually want to envisage. It was something that you understood in school all right. If you said you were going to do something, you kept your word on it.

I think, 'my word is my bond' had another side to it. When you joined the City and you realized that your most important asset is your good name, that had all the old connotations of honour, trust, complete integrity, that was the most important thing you could do. You could take years building up a good name and you could lose it in one transaction. Again the ethos of the public school.

There were a lot of conventions, of course, in the Stock Exchange and in the City in those early days. One was dress. As a partner I always had to wear a bowler hat and carry a rolled umbrella when in the street. If you didn't have your bowler hat on and carry your umbrella you weren't properly dressed as a stockbroker. And then, of course, came the question of whether you were wearing a hard white collar or not. If you wore a striped shirt, the other members of the Stock Exchange would crowd round shouting 'Pyjamas, pyjamas.' If you were smartly turned out in a conventional way, again that was part of the trust. You were somebody that people could deal with and you were a gentleman, and that was in your favour.

It was very, very important that you should be seen to be behaving like a gentleman and that you should comport yourself like a gentleman, and then people could trust you and deal with you.

CHAPTER FIVE

The Lover

———————— • ————————

In September 1946 seventeen-year-old Roy Booth went to his girlfriend Betty's house in Neston near Birkenhead to tell her mother that she was pregnant:

Betty's mother cried and she called me some awful names, she said, 'I'm ashamed of you, you've brought disgrace on my family. I trusted you Roy and look what you've done.' She said, 'Does your family know?'

Strict codes of etiquette had to be observed when boy met girl at the dancehall.

•

Above: *An illustration from 'How and What to Dance', an instruction manual on etiquette, written in 1906, which stressed the importance of 'gentlemanly behaviour' for young men.*

Right: *Roy Booth pictured in the early 1950s. After marrying Betty in 1946 the couple went on to have four children and are still happily married.*

The last waltz at a dance in the early 1950s. Dance halls were the place for young people to meet and fall in love during this era.

•

I said, 'No'.

She said, 'Well, they're going to,' and she put on a coat and we walked up to my house.

My father said, 'What's this?'

I said, 'I've got something to tell you.'

Betty's mother interrupted, 'I'll tell him, he's got my daughter pregnant.'

So my father he just went berserk, he said, 'I've always said you were bloody thick, what have you gone and done this for?' When he'd cooled down he said, 'Get married quick so people in Neston won't know.'

•

In the immediate post-war years romance and respectability were bolted together almost as firmly as they had been in Victorian times. For many decades young couples had been pushed into shotgun weddings to avoid the stigma of a bastard child. Most of the blame – and responsibility for the consequences – was generally shouldered by the young woman who had consented to sex before marriage. But it was thought proper that the man, too, should pay his dues and do the decent thing, for he had broken the rules of courtship befitting an English gentleman.

The ideal of gentlemanly behaviour towards the opposite sex and the observation of an elaborate code of etiquette in the company of a 'young lady' permeated all levels of society during the first half of the century. It was a brand of Christian manliness advocated by practically all of the most influential youth movements and organizations of the time – the Boy Scouts, the YMCA, youth clubs and so on. The importance of behaving like a gentleman also formed the backbone of most courtship and sex education manuals. It was given an injection of glamour by a host of feature films celebrating the chivalrous hero. *Knight Without Armour* (1937) starred Robert Donat – the perfect English gentleman and the British cinema's undisputed romantic leading man of the 1930s. However, what the chivalric ideal meant in practice for the ordinary couple was rather more mundane. The romance would, in its early stages, be vetted by both sets of parents – often over Sunday tea – for the suitability of the match. Most preferred not to take too many risks, choosing a partner from a similar background who was steady and reliable and who (from the man's viewpoint) seemed likely to make a good housekeeper and mother. Few of the men we interviewed felt able to tell their partner that they loved them. To do so would have been an embarrassing and decidedly unEnglish show of emotion.

There was often a lengthy period of engagement (whilst saving for a home), a strong disapproval of sex before marriage, and a high age of marriage. During the Edwardian era the average age of marriage was higher than at any other moment in British history, peaking at twenty-seven years for men and twenty-six for women. What was looked forward to most of all was the romantic climax to the courtship – the increasingly popular 'white wedding' which celebrated the virgin bride, then the honeymoon night when the couple (supposedly) had sex for the first time. According to Ted Cunningham, who married in 1932, the wedding night was 'the best moment of your life, that first night that you had sex with your missus.' For some we interviewed, however, the wedding night was a spectacular disaster as neither partner knew what to do. The men who took the gentlemanly ideal most to heart – a few aspiring to be a latterday version of the medieval knight – tended to be from a lower-middle or middle-class background, men who, like Sidney Ling, had been given a formal training as 'little gentlemen' from a very young age.

The courtship rituals of this new breed of gentlemen were acted out every night of the week on dance floors up and down the country. Bert Barnes, the son of a gardener in Paddington, remembers the atmosphere of the sixpenny hops in North London in the 1920s:

•

We used to dress up for them. I remember my own dress consisted of tomato-red Oxford bags which had to be thirty-six inches round the bottom and a tight jacket with loads of buttons down the front and possibly a pork pie hat or an umbrella. We dressed smartly. And the ladies, they used to preen themselves, usually their dress was a long ballgown, with gold or silver shoes. The general sort of address when you wanted to dance was 'May I have the pleasure of this dance', and she would invariably agree. Seldom did she say no, probably if you were half drunk she might, but we never used to go half drunk to a dance, we'd try to act as gentlemen, I do recall going to the Caxton House restaurant one night and there you were expected to wear white gloves because the ladies had nice white dresses and if your hands got a bit sweaty you didn't want to make an impression on the lady's ballgown. There was a certain etiquette about dancing in those days.'

•

But there were limits to gentlemanly behaviour. Beneath the chivalrous veneer often lay more basic male instincts of sexual desire and possession. When they surfaced – triggered for example by competition for girls – there could be violence. Bert Barnes recalls: 'Inevitably there were scraps on the dance floor. You had your designs on one particular girl and possibly others had the same idea, and it was a generally accepted thing to warn him off and if he didn't appreciate his warning you used to hit him. Sometimes you knew the opponent and other times you didn't. You were looking after

Bert and Doris Barnes in the late 1920s.
The couple met at a dance in Willesden,
North London, in 1925.

•

British soldiers depart for France in 1940. Long years of separation were a testing time for many relationships – the divorce rate doubled during the war.

•

your own. It was manly to look after your girls and they appreciated it. You were their hero and you went up a peg.'

It was accepted that a gentleman had strong sexual urges and if he failed to contain them — as was thought to be natural from time to time — it was the duty of the young lady to resist. When a young man's sexual advances were rejected his frustration was often tempered by a satisfaction that he had found a woman who was worthy of his love and marriage. The virginity of the bride-to-be was for many men a sacred part of the courtship ritual. However, there was such widespread ignorance and fear of sex that even in moments of high passion between lovers, the young woman's moral purity was often not put to the test. When Humphrey Gillett went courting on country walks in the 1930s his amorous ambitions always fell short of full sex.

Where young men did have sex on a one-night stand or in a short-term relationship it was usually seen in terms of male sexual conquest and the age-old 'sowing of wild oats'. In these relationships the pretence of love and romance was seen by some men as very important in persuading a young woman to have sex. As a young man in the 1930s Bob Tindale, a miner in the Durham pit village of High Spen, prided himself on his sexual conquests. His success, he believed, was in no small part due to his 'gift of the gab' and his ability to croon the popular romantic songs of the day to the girls on the local 'chicken run' – the street where boys and girls met at weekends. 'When you went out you started to sing walking down the street, "I'm no millionaire, but I'm not the type to care, 'cos I've got a pocketful of dreams", you know, in the Crosby style. And she'd say, "you're a good singer". You kept singing and showing yourself off to them, sort of boasting, until you did catch one and that was the name of the game, and you'd be well away.'

At the beginning of the Second World War there appeared to be a great blossoming of love and romance, with a marriage boom in which three out of every ten brides were under twenty-one. But most of the young couples who pledged lifelong fidelity barely knew each other. The young men who rushed into these wartime weddings, like Humphrey Gillett and Albert Gomes, were very conscious of the fact that they might die soon and in this uncertain atmosphere marriage offered the attractions of a sacred and romantic ritual, sex and a widow's pension for their wives should the worst happen. To begin with, most couples seem to have been faithful but after a few years a considerable number of these wartime marriages had begun to founder. There was a mood of living for the present and many husbands formed loving relationships with local women or women serving alongside them in the armed forces. Most tried to keep their affairs secret, which was much easier for men serving in another country than for their wives back home who were under the constant scrutiny of neighbours and relatives. Right up to the present, men in the armed forces have been more reluctant than women to talk about wartime affairs and, as a consequence, far more is known about adultery on the home front than overseas.

After the war it had been widely assumed that relationships between the sexes would return to normal and couples would settle down to the old domestic routine. But there were often serious problems of adjustment. Gay men, like Tony Kildwick, uncertain and confused about their sexuality, felt pressurized into marriage – often with disastrous consequences. Some returning soldiers, like Frank Davies, a Japanese prisoner of war for three years in the Far East, felt physically and emotionally shattered and to begin with found relationships with young women very difficult.

Young men and women who had been used to more sexual freedom during the war found it hard suddenly to give it up. Ray Turner, married in 1946, remembers his anger at an affair his wife had shortly afterwards: 'A friend tipped me off it was happening in this field so we went behind this hedge and hid. A car came up along the road and stopped and they started canoodling. I said "eeh, that's my missus." He said "told ya" and by this time they'd got to it, they were having sex. I went round the hedge and said, "I'm Ray Turner fra' Preston and I happen to be her husband." Bang, and I gave him such a clout, poor fellow went flat.' Ray and his wife split up soon afterwards.

The number of divorces rocketed to what was then the highest-ever figure of 60 000 in 1947. Some, like Albert Gomes, stuck with unhappy marriages made during the war for the sake of the children. Thirty-five years went by before he felt able to divorce and marry the love of his life.

By then the old romantic ideal of marriage as a lifelong bond and duty had worn thin, even for couples who had courted before the war. Albert was part of a new trend in which older people have taken advantage of the more liberal attitudes towards divorce and sexuality. It is perhaps because of this change in attitude that the men whose testimonies follow have felt able to talk so honestly about their relationships and to say things that would have been thought very shocking fifty years ago.

Geordie Todd

•

Geordie and Ellen went to the same school in North Shields. They started courting as teenagers and married in 1935. Geordie was extremely candid in the interview, and had decided to talk openly about his marriage and wartime affairs for the first time. He wanted tapes of the unedited interview to give to his two granddaughters. Despite the upheaval of the Second World War, Geordie and Ellen remained happily married until her death in 1972. Her final words to him were 'I love you Geordie'.

•

Her name was Ellie Bonnet. I'd known her when I was at school, and we got on talking and after a while I just asked her to go to the pictures and she agreed. I think we had the pictures four or five times before we settled to go regular, to court regular. At the finish I just said to her, 'Well, are we going together proper?' And that was it. I was introduced to her mother and father and after that I was a regular visitor.

It was all conversational mostly. She would talk about what she had done since I had last seen her and I would tell her about what happened at sea. I think it was twelve months before we could even get close. She was, 'Oh no, don't come too close to us George.' Stand-offish. When we stood at her front door, she was standing in the door and I maybe a yard from her and it was a quick peck on the lips and, 'Goodnight George, I'll see you next trip.' That was it.

I still had to be in for ten o'clock at night at me lodgings. I've seen me with the last minute, and scatter up them stairs two at a time.

There was one time I was at a twenty-first birthday party and I got a few drinks, which I'd never done, and the next day when I told her she says, 'You can cut that out. I think too much of ya for you to go

Geordie and Ellen Todd on their wedding day.
Ellen's dress was pink as she especially wanted a 'pink wedding'.

drinking and I'd rather you didn't.' I says, 'Fair enough.' I never had any more to drink, ever, till the war broke out. 'Course it was done then, you weren't a tough guy unless you could hold your drink sort of style.

We had been going together for about fourteen months and you know, when you're kissing and cuddling you try to slide your hand across her and 'whack' – clip across lug and, 'Any more of that and you've had it George.' You didn't try any more. She was the girl I wanted, the only one I really settled on.

It showed me a great respect for her, she was wanting to keep herself pure and untouched till the day she got married. That's why I became more attached to her. I just thought to meself, 'Well, if she doesn't want me, if she's not going to let me, she won't let anybody else, sort of style.' I respected that, I thought the world of her.

She was everything I looked for, pretty and bonny. I looked up to her almost like a Madonna to me and I felt as if I just wanted to care for her. She'd walk round the fish quay and see us landing and she'd stand and talk to us while I was landing the fish like. 'Are you off tonight?'

'No, I'm sailing again at one o'clock.'

'Oh, well, I'm going to the dance tonight. What about a treat.'

I'd say, 'no.' Then of course she'd say she'd get someone else to take her then naturally me hand went in me pocket and you give her a treat to the dance, although you weren't there.

In the latter part just before we got married, we used to cuddle and kiss and I used to say, 'By crikey, I don't half love you.' She'd say, 'Well, it goes two ways George, I love you.'

The day we got married I'd just come in from sea on the Saturday morning and me sister had everything laid out on the bed, ready for us. She was dressed in pink and I was waiting in the church with me best man, a fellow from the boat. When I saw her coming down the aisle on her father's arm I thought, 'Oh blimey, I've never seen her like that before, so beautiful.'

We had a little flat and that night we sat talking and I said, 'Well, are we going to bed?' But she made me undress in the living-room while she went in the bedroom. Fair enough, so after a while I went into the bedroom and she was lying in bed. I got into bed with her and she says, 'This is the part I'm not going to like'. And I says, 'This is the part I hope I to enjoy.' 'Course, it was a fiasco. She had never had

Geordie Todd in Durban, South Africa in 1943 during his Navy Service.

•

anything to do with sex and this was only my sixth or seventh time. I had to sail the next morning and cook says, 'What's the matter? You went at it too much last night.' I says, 'I didn't get a bloody chance.' I was trying to explain to him and he said I must have rushed things too much.

We finished the trip and came in and so that night we took things very easy and that was a very successful night. After that we had no trouble though some trips we came in I was too tired, it was just a case of getting to bed and having a good sleep, ready for sailing the next day again. Years later many a time, the wife used to sit in the chair over there and I used to sit in the chair there and used to remember these things, our wedding night. We just laughed about it.

I was six years away during the war. I told the wife. I says, 'I'm going away abroad and I'll be away two year at least.' She shed a few tears and when I left home that morning she wanted to come to Newcastle Station to see us off. But I said for her to stay at home. I never saw her no more for three years and two months.

You tried to be a faithful husband but it was impossible to be 'cos you were living on a knife edge the whole time you were at sea and when you came in at Durban or Cape Town there was always women there waiting for you, to take you away for the day and you did get involved. I never went with a prostitute. I had an arrangement. I was in the Mayfair Hotel in Durban and this woman came, late twenties, and got talking like and the next thing we knew she'd invited us to her home and her and I kept company right till the day I sailed for home. We had a good relationship and, yes, I think she shed a few tears when I left her. She knew that it was only a wartime sort of romance. She had two little girls and when I left there I just said to her, 'Well this is the end of a perfect relationship.' She said she'd never forget me.

When I arrived home that day the wife said, 'I don't want to know anything of what you did while you were away. That's yours and keep it to yourself, end of story.' We just started life from there on again. I think in her own heart she knew a married man couldn't go three year without having a sexual relationship with a woman but she never really enquired about what happened. I thought about it often, of this woman that I'd left there.

Sidney Ling

•

Sidney is tall and upright, the reward of a youth spent religiously keeping fit and exercising. He lives in a small modern house with his wife Gwen on the outskirts of Woodbridge, Suffolk. The rooms are decorated with his paintings of local scenes. After a career spent in teaching, and twenty years as a headmaster, he has returned to the county where he was born in 1910. Sidney met Gwen at the local tennis club in July 1934. They married in 1938. Their two sons, Howard and Graham, were born in 1941 and 1944 while Sidney was serving in the RAF.

•

Sidney Ling (right) with a friend in the early 1930s. They were keen swimmers and even tried to learn to dive like Johnny Weismuller, the actor who played Tarzan.

•

I always had my cap on, my school cap and a little walking stick with a silver knob. I was trained to be a little gentleman and raise my hat to the ladies which you always had to do, you see, and if I didn't do it father would be after me. We were trained along those lines, to be gentlemen, and to be courteous to people, to speak properly, and not to slang. We were brought up in a strict family and my father and mother were strict and smart.

Before I got the scholarship I was at the local council school at Hadleigh for a year and a bit and Dilys was also at that school. I was about eight or nine and the headmaster, who was a great musician, he taught us the song, 'Winter is gone and the springtime is here.' And that put me in a right romantic mood and there was Dilys sitting like an angel on the other side of the class looking lovely and I sort of fell in love with Dilys. She lived out of town about three miles and cycled in. Well, she just fascinated me, she was a lovely girl and I was deeply in love with her but she never knew and I never did speak with her. I was dead scared of her.

One has long, long dreams of romance and one wonders when one's princess will come along and she was my princess at that time. They were quite classy people and they lived in a beautiful house so she was a cut above me. I thought that but I still loved her and she remained very aloof of the other girls, she wasn't a ragtag bobtail kind of girl, she was elegant. She walked like a princess, she spoke like a princess, she looked like a princess, and I loved her, but she never knew it.

But I used to walk up to where she lived and pick primroses and cowslips intending to give them to her as a token of my love. But I never did, I used to finish by taking them home to Mum and trying to explain why I was late for tea. But even to this day I remember Dilys as being very like a princess with lovely deportment, very elevated. She was different from the other girls.

But then when Dilys came to the grammar school she, of course, went to the girls' department and I went to the boys' department and never the twain shall meet, so I didn't see much of her except when she sat in the back seat looking all demure and lovely.

But as a young boy I was very, very meek and unassuming and afraid, especially of girls. I worshipped them but only from afar. I think that I developed along the lines of what might be called a genteel man. If I may presume to liken myself to a flower garden I think I burgeoned out into manhood like flowers do, with many, many strings to my development. Sport, physique, swimming, tennis, music, showing off to the girls, you see.

I was a very romantic fellow. I fantasied over lovely, lovely girls but I was still afraid of 'em. We had our dances and of course there was no drink and we'd have our girls there. They'd be at one end and we'd be at the other end, all coy and smart. They'd all have their pretty little dresses on, and we were perhaps dared to go and ask a girl to dance. It was quite a challenge and I was never brave enough.

I didn't spend an awful lot of time going out with young women because I had other fish to fry like exams to pass and so on, and football to play. But I was always mindful that that little bit of feminity was different from me. Where women were concerned I looked upon them as something apart, something almost sacred. Some of them would make advances to me which once again I wasn't quite certain about, in an embrace, you know, and I wasn't quite certain what they were angling for. I think I could have gone crazy over girls and gone a long way with girls had I had the nerve but God didn't give me the nerve so I behaved decently.

*Above: Sidney and Gwen Ling on their
wedding day in August 1938.*

*Right: Sidney and Gwen at the christen-
ing of their youngest son Graham who
was born in 1944.*

•

Then Gwen came along. She joined the tennis club so I got to know her quite well and we played tennis together and we made a thing of it because she lived at Streatham and I was teaching in London and we'd do our courting in the West End. We'd go into the gods for ninepence, we'd go into Hyde Park for a tanner, have a couple of deckchairs and listen to the band, that sort of thing, but I always tried to maintain a courtly behaviour. I always think the female sex warranted that.

We used to go to the cinema of course and see romantic films, and I remember pinching a handkerchief of Gwen's, a little silk handkerchief it was, a pink one, and I kept that for donkey's years until it rotted away, you know, all the way through the war and just the smell of that reminded me of Gwen.

When we were courting we did go to the Isle of Wight for a holiday before we were married, and we stayed in a boarding house. We had separate bedrooms of course but I'd go into Gwen's bedroom at night and kiss her goodnight and then disappear, honestly. You see because you didn't know anything about contraception or anything, I'd got no clue about what one did with a girl. So we had our holiday and I can't say more than that. We went to this concert and that concert, we did a lot of swimming in the sea, we went walking over the downs. Sex didn't rear its ugly head at all really when I was courting Gwen. I was interested in her but not to that extent. I just didn't know.

It was very embarrassing on our honeymoon, very embarrassing. We just didn't, you know. Gwen didn't want to and she was afraid anyway and I didn't know much about it. So it was just an embarrassing fortnight and that went on for quite a bit afterwards. You see you'd never talked about it with a girl, you'd never dare, and mothers and fathers never discussed it with their children. Mother never told me anything, nor did Dad.

Then all of a sudden, of course, Howard was on the way in the spring of 1941. He was born just before Christmas 1941 and that was that. I don't know how he got born, really, but there we were in this brand new house, brand new married, a year.

But I felt so guilty that Gwen was having to go through this at a time when the future was so unsure for us all. We'd got no future, the war was there and we were going to get hell. I'd probably be put up against a wall and shot, or sent to Germany for forced labour and Gwen would be probably....oh, all sorts of things, and that was the beginning of our married life and I didn't feel pleased with myself at all.

I had to join up and so I couldn't be at home. I couldn't be with her you see. I was in the Air Force, didn't go overseas but I might as well have done, but I did feel very sorry for her because she was alone in Yorkshire, with this little baby, only a fortnight old and I was posted up to Scotland. There she was coping with a little baby, and of course the same happened again later, everything was all upsy down-sy in 1943 when our second son came along, Graham. I felt so sorry, so guilty that I got a compassionate posting home.

Albert Gomes

•

Albert has lived alone since he was widowed. The modern bungalow he lives in on the outskirts of Liverpool is meticulously kept. Albert too is very smartly dressed, a softly spoken, gentle man. He married Beatrice in 1941 and they had a daughter in 1942 and a son in 1947. He met and fell in love with Betty in 1949, but decided to stay in his first marriage because of the children, and Betty married somebody else. They met again twenty-nine years later, and they married in 1982. They had ten happy years together before she died.

•

We were getting ready for going overseas, so I thought, 'Oh well I'll probably get killed here, won't be coming back, so I'll do her a favour I'll marry her and at least she will get the widow's allowance.' Really speaking, it was very unfair to get married on that basis, it wasn't the ideal way to start a relationship but that's how we got married.

'Course nothing happened to me at all and after the war I came home and we put our names down for a council house which I was entitled to as a serviceman. We had a little daughter and in February 1947 the wife gave birth to a son. It was what I considered normal. I sort of got into a pattern of living with her and obviously I had affec-tion for her, but I was never really in love.

I got this job in a garage which entailed me talking on the tele-phone to customers about their vehicles and times to collect and times to bring them in and so forth. Well, I used to spend quite a lot

Betty, the love of Albert Gomes' life, photographed on her wedding day in 1950. Albert finally married Betty thirty-two years later.

•

of time talking to this lady on the other end of the telephone, Betty. She worked at one of the other offices and we got quite a good relationship going, in fact I'm falling in love with her and I haven't even seen her.

We started talking when it wasn't to do with work and I found out she was engaged to a chap who lived in Newton le Willows and she only saw him at weekends so all the week she was sort of free. I'd built a picture up in my mind of the person she was and she came across as a very, very nice person.

One day at work the chaps were looking at these horses in the paper to pick on to back and there was one called Fleeting Moment. It sort of struck a chord because my relationship with Betty was a sort of fleeting moment, never seen her, it was just the talking and I had a few bob in my pocket saved. So I put a pound on it each way and of course I told Betty during the course of speaking to her later on, that I'd done this. She said, 'Oh it's twenty-eight to one, what are you going to do with all the money if you win?' And I said I'd take her out. It was sort of half-joking and half-hoping she would accept.

Well, Fleeting Moment won and that was how we made our first date. She said, 'Yes' and we met outside the Odeon Cinema in Waterloo. I'm standing outside and I saw a young lady standing the other side. I thought, 'That's a cracker.' It was Betty, so that was it, I was well gone then.

That was in November and it went on getting ever more involved and we met twice a week when I was meant to be at the TAs. It was a different ball game to my marriage. I was head over heels, straight in, right over the top and I'd never known anything like it. I've only ever had those feelings once in my life, I don't think you could ever have them twice, I don't think it's possible to get those feelings twice because you would never be able to reach that depth of experiences. I was thirty-one years of age and I knew the difference then between physical attraction and really caring for somebody, really loving somebody.

It went on for a couple of months and got far more intense and then we did have a physical relationship, that was February. By that time I could only think of one person, Betty. And I knew she was coming up for getting married in March, March 17th.

I kept putting it on the back burner, knowing all the time that time was running out and it came to the Thursday before she was getting married on the Saturday, so we met again. We just went into a park which was open and we sat in the park shelter and we talked and we cried and we talked. She begged and prayed of me not to let her marry, she would do anything, go away with me, whatever and I was very tempted to, very tempted, it was the hardest decision I ever made in my life to have to turn her down because I loved her so much. It was just an impossible situation I was in. You see I was absolutely devoted to my children, absolutely, thought the world of them, and I tried in every way possible to make up to them whatever feelings I had of being deprived of a father when I was young. I couldn't leave them as I'd been left by my father. I'd promised myself. But I can't describe what a torture it was to have to decide between the children and giving Betty up, to have to say 'goodbye' to her that night. Emotionally we were both drained, we cried and held each other until almost light.

I went home at three o'clock in the morning, opened the door, and the wife was there, 'Where the hell have you been?' I was that distraught I didn't give a bugger so I told her the whole story and then we sat talking right through to half-past seven the next morning.

I was absolutely living in another world from that day. On Saturday the wife went to Betty's wedding and I was desperate in case she caused a fuss and caused any hassle. But anyway, she just went as a spectator and came back and gave me some more earache but by that time I was past caring. I wasn't concerned about her feelings because mine were so traumatic. She even hit me over the head with a hammer and I couldn't have cared less 'cos all I could see was Betty marrying someone else when that was the last thing in the world I wanted.

There was just a blank for years and years and years. Although we

Albert Gomes with his two children.
Albert's own father deserted the family when Albert was only a few years old.
•

slept in the same bed I didn't touch my wife physically. In fact the last time I'd done it I felt so disgusted with myself that I felt physically unclean, you know. I had to have a wash, a bath, it was as if I couldn't wash myself clean enough to get this lousy feeling off me and I never touched her once from that time. I couldn't have looked Betty in the face anyway, if I had done. I couldn't have watched meself shave in the morning and gone to Betty knowing that I'd done that.

We used to go out at weekends to the pub. They were singing pubs, so you could go out and have a good singsong and a few drinks. And I used to sit watching the door and when the door opened keep hoping against hope that Betty would walk in. She never did, of course, but I kept hoping she would. She was always at the back of my mind.

It was twenty-nine years later that I had a telephone call from Betty. She knew my children would be grown up by then and I know now that she'd been thinking of me just as much as I had of her. So we started meeting again, all those years after, but even then

Albert Gomes pictured in the 1950s. Despite his decision to stay with his family, Albert never forgot his love for Betty.

still in secret. We would spend two hours together in a car park snogging and talking and whatever and that went on for two years. I couldn't ask her, then, to do something I wasn't prepared to do and that was to leave her husband. Although her children was well gone by then. I just couldn't ask her to do that because he was in bad health. I thought far too much about her to put her in that situation, so I didn't do that.

Then one night the telephone rings, one o'clock in the morning. It was Betty telling me that Tom had died. Obviously I couldn't do anything about it at one o'clock in the morning so I made arrangements to go and see her the next day. I supported her as much as I could under the circumstances and then, of course, when I came home my wife wanted to know where I'd been, what I'd been up to. I told her and it led to a furious row, as you can well imagine. I decided then, 'Well, that's it. I'm not putting up with this situation and I don't have to now.'

Betty wanted me to come and live with her but she was afraid of what the neighbours might say, 'cos her husband hadn't been dead that long, it was only like a matter of a month, six weeks. She didn't think it was right, nor did I, so I stayed on this caravan site for a couple of months or more. Then one night she said, 'Oh, to hell with the neighbours, it's ridiculous that you're over here and we want to be living together.' It went from there and then of course the divorce proceedings had started and my wife made all sorts of allegations about what a swine I was, kept her short of money, this, that and the other. I could have shot her down in flames, but I wanted a divorce and so I kept quiet.

The divorce came through the day before we actually got married and a day later we went on our honeymoon. We couldn't have done it any quicker. It was a privilege, the happiest years of my life. We had ten years together. It really did destroy me for a while when Betty died. She'd always been the only person I've ever really loved.

Humphrey Gillett

•

Humphrey was wearing a wide-rimmed hat and a red blouson, a mark of his individuality. He worked for many years as a headmaster in schools both in England and abroad. His willingness to talk openly about love and sex is rare for a man of his generation. He claims, 'sex is never better than when you are in your seventies.' He met his wife-to-be, Janet, on a cycling holiday in Sussex in 1939, and they have been married for fifty-five years. They have four children and seven grand-children. They live in a small modern bungalow in a quiet cul-de-sac in Fairford, Gloucestershire.

•

As a young man I felt that until I'd had a full sexual experience I was not grown up – that was a rite of passage. But I was too scared really.

Youth Hostels were a good mating ground and the general aim was to meet girls. You paid a shilling a night and you cooked your own food. It was a cheap way of seeing the countryside. We used to cycle miles from hostel to hostel. There was a sense in which the

Humphrey and Janet Gillett in the 1940s on a walking holiday.

•

English countryside acquired an almost magical or spiritual significance. I used to love to cycle to the top of the North Downs and gaze across the Weald of Kent. I loved the independence of it, it gave me freedom and that's what it's all about.

I didn't say, 'I wonder what is the best youth hostel to meet an attractive girl.' That was just by accident. I didn't plan it in any way, it was just exploring, going to new places on my bicycle. But inevitably meeting girls was one of the things you did at the hostels and I thought it was a very attractive thing too.

I had some of my early experiences on those holidays. I mean, bracken does make a very nice hidey place if you want to make love to a girl. You can pull it right over you. But in my case they were near experiences. I could never quite go the whole way. In any case, having penetrated and had full sex with a women, you felt that you then belonged to her and she belonged to you, I mean it wasn't just shaking hands. It was a fact that you were more closely bound than you would possibly wish to be at that stage. So I think it was trying not to be entangled and trying to retain my freedom and also trying in a sense to have your cake and eat it.

I viewed women as beautiful creatures with a higher degree of sensitivity to ourselves, as being a prize to be won, shall we say. On the other hand there was a sense in which they were out to capture you and there was a sense you tried to avoid being captured.

You felt that you were invading a woman's privacy as indeed you would be and if you weren't totally committed to her you shouldn't do it. Women would sort of hint, by inference, that they were sexually available, but they didn't give you practical guidance. It was totally an element of selfishness, driven by sexual need, on the other hand inhibited by fear of pregancy, by fear of gonorrhoea, syphilis, by fear of hurting a women, by fear of not fulfilling an obligation which you had entered into by penetrating the woman's vagina.

I was extremely fond of Plato's *Republic* at the time and I felt the way to woo a woman was to get her to read Plato's *Republic,* and so when I met Janet I suggested that perhaps she might like to borrow it. So she gave me her address in London and I went round to have tea with her. The friendship started there and it was quite a romantic friendship in the beginning.

In 1939 we sewed two blankets together so we'd be together and we put a pentacle of red ribbon on the top which she sewed and we went out and slept on the top of Dry Hill in Surrey for the night. Nothing happened really, it was not that sort of relationship at the time and once again the old inhibitions came up. It wasn't a full relationship at all until we were married, a full sexual relationship.

After I'd joined the Army I was in deep despair. The life was tough and I knew it. The training and the regime was harsh and I had the prospect of years of it, living with these other men who all seemed

Humphrey and Janet Gillett shortly after they met in 1939.
Their great hobby was walking and cycling in the countryside.

much more suited to the military life. I was stationed in Yeovil, wandering round one day, when suddenly Janet appeared in the High Street. She'd come to see me and she came to tell me to be a man and get on with it and not moan so much. That was very much Janet really and I made her a ring out of grass and put it on her finger as we sat there and we had another bond between us.

When I was in France I wrote and asked her to stand on the leeward side of a beech tree during the autumn when it was shedding its leaves and capture two leaves and she did. She had to catch them before they touched the ground and we kept a leaf for many, many years, as a sort of bond between us.

The courtship was extremely short. By the end of September I was abroad and we got married during my first leave, which was in January 1940. Somebody said, 'You're almost certain to be killed in this war and if you have a girlfriend the sensible thing is to marry her.' In a sense it was looking for fulfilment since it seemed only too likely that I wouldn't survive.

Sex really didn't happen properly until I came back from Dunkirk and then she became quite a camp follower and because she was a very attractive girl of course my status in the unit went up. I had the use of a lorry and I used to smuggle her in.

But once the first child is born you've really lost your wife, it's how it seemed to me. I don't see a lot of difference between a person being a wife and a person being a prostitute in those days. I mean the wife was selling her body for the upkeep of her children. It was a contract wasn't it? They were being driven by the genetic needs to pass their genes on, the same as men were and my feelings is birth, copulation and death, that's what life is about, and marriage and engagements and wedding cakes and bridal dresses and that sort of thing are nothing to do with it. I was driven by the need to copulate and the women were driven by the need to copulate and produce children and that's what it comes down to. I think that's the basic contract and all the other is just the fripperies. I felt that the children came to dominate the marriage rather than her relationship with me. I was very hurt when I drew lots to come home from India on leave and she wrote and said that it was just as well I couldn't come because the children were at a difficult stage or something. I'd been in India for eighteen months and I wanted to go home, to be with her and make love to her. I'd been faithful to her in India and I did feel rejected. That was deeply hurtful and probably the marriage never really fully recovered. So after the war she wanted her own bed. We were more friends than lovers really.

So I did have an affair with a deputy headmistress whom I taught to drive. I had affairs that didn't result in going to bed but I found women attractive. I mean it's 'hogamous, higamous, men are polygamous, higamous, hogamous, women are monogamous.'

I probably did feel a sense of guilt but not at a very deep level. I did feel that I had been rejected by Janet and that other husbands had a closer relationship with their wives than I had. I still needed the close relationship with womankind but I haven't wished to have one-night stands which I never had. I was looking for the love and the sexual fulfilment that was lacking in my marriage. Yes, I think that is true because Janet laid down very firm rules about sex. I might be given it from time to time if I was good but never during the day.

But I don't love Janet any less because I've had affairs with other women. Women seemed to be prepared to put up with me for a time, but I'm inclined to think that the longer they know me the less they like me. I think they find me in the end rather unsatisfactory. I still like it when a passionate lover, mistress, affair, becomes a friend-ship and lasts, and that is what has happened in several instances.

She usually found out, yes, you can't keep much from a woman. They're very perceptive creatures and we did have arguments. She's been very angry, but we still stayed together. I mean I did once say to her that, in future, I would not be inhibited sexually, if I had the opportunity and if she didn't like it then we could have a divorce, but she chose to stay with me.

Tony Kildwick

•

Tony describes himself as being 'a conventional young man' during his time at Cambridge University just after the last war. He married because he believed it was the right thing to do, and it was only later in life that he finally confronted his true sexual identity. He was involved in early campaigns for gay rights, in the days before gay liberation became part of the vocabulary. He was separated from his wife in 1974, and he now lives in a shared house with other gay men.

•

I never for one moment thought of myself as being gay. There was one boy at school who I had a very, very close relationship with. He was a clever actor, an artist, very amusing, and I used to invite him to come on holidays but the idea of going to bed with him absolute-ly never entered either of our heads.

I mean, one masturbated, but I personally masturbated with a sort of male fantasy in my mind. Certain handsome men turned me on and I thought this was perfectly normal, I didn't in any way have a particularly guilty feeling about it. I thought, 'Well, perhaps every-body goes through this thing.' One was so innocent in those days.

This was how I was, it was me. I reacted in this way, and it never really troubled me. What troubled me much more I think was mas-turbating, because the fear that masturbating was going to send you mad had been instilled into us at school. That's what caused the guilt feeling, not the feeling that I was emotionally and, to some extent, sexually attracted to men.

I just thought that, you know, there was some nice handsome boy

*Tony Kildwick with a school friend
shortly before he went up to Cambridge in 1938.*

●

and if I wanted to masturbate I wanted to think about somebody, I'd think about him. I knew I was not effeminate, I didn't like dressing up in female clothes, I wasn't a transvestite. I wasn't in the least bit attracted in either reality or in fantasy to men dressed as women, in fact I rather disliked it and still do. But I was very much attracted by very masculine men and I thought of myself as a masculine man. The fact that you could be gay and, you know, very masculine, just never entered into one's head.

I mean sex was discussed in general terms, about what did you do when you went to bed with a tart. I certainly got this thought that, 'Well, there'll come a time when I'll marry and it'll be all right. I shall do my duty and become a father,' It never occurred to me at that

162

Tony Kildwick as a student of Modern Languages. His degree was interrupted by the Second World War and he was only able to return to finish the course in 1947.

stage that this wouldn't happen automatically.

I went back up to Cambridge and quite early on in the term I was invited to go and have tea in the master's lodge as most newly returned undergraduates were. It was there that I met a girl. In fact I had known her when we were children. We'd both been to the same dancing class as kids and we'd lost contact. But she recognized my name and I reconized her and, well, we fell in love.

I'm very family-conscious: The oldest son of the oldest son of the oldest son going back for many generations, and I obviously thought that it was my duty to get married. Everybody else in my family had got married and everybody else had produced children and I thought that I would do the same. It never occurred to me to do differently, I mean, I was a very conventional young man.

There was a pressure to prove one's manhood and to prove yourself not a wimp. You had to show that you were able and capable of doing manly things. So I was thinking in terms of what all the rest of my contemporaries were doing, which was to marry, settle down. I met a girl with whom I shared an enormous amount in common and I just fell in love with her. Not physically, perhaps but intellectually and in every way. One's sexuality was simply not discussed and not understood. I don't think that I was any less in love than if I'd been rampaging to go to bed with her.

I asked her to marry me and she accepted but before we got married I thought it was prudent to go and consult a doctor, because I was a virgin. I'd never had sex with a woman before, I wanted just to get clued up. I was as innocent as the driven snow in that respect, but I also was worried at that stage that all my fantasies were male fantasies. So I went and I saw the doctor in Cambridge, who knew my fiancée. The first question he asked me was what was I reading and I said I was reading Modern Languages. He said, 'Oh well, if you're not

The Lover

an artist and you're not effeminate, you can't be homosexual.' And he said, 'Well, you've been to public school, you've been in the Army, you've never had any contact with women, it's hardly surprising that you should have this sort of thing. But don't worry, she's a damn nice girl, it'll be all right on the night.' I accepted that.

Everybody was saying, 'This is the marriage of the decade, you know, here you are, your families are going to be united.' Everybody was happy about it.

The honeymoon was pretty ghastly. First of all we went to Ireland and the first night was spent on a very rough boat crossing the Irish Sea. We sort of toured round Ireland and it just didn't work. I mean, it was dreadful. We tried and or I tried and I'd rather not go into it, I mean, it was just catastrophic, looking back, from both our points of view. You see we put it down to the fact that nine people out of ten in those days always expected to have a rough start. The girls didn't really know what to expect and the chaps had never been taught.

Both of us were virgins. We knew in theory what we had to do but I didn't get particularly excited or aroused by her. She was obviously nervous and frightened as to what was going to happen to her because we lived in that kind of ignorance.

Gradually, during that time, I became more and more and more convinced that things were, well, I was certain, that things were not as they should be. By that time we'd moved to another part of the country and I was farming at the time. Our doctor became a very great personal friend so I went to him and I said, 'Now look, this is the problem, I get no sexual satisfaction at all in my married life. I still have these male fantasies, d'you think I'm homosexual?' And he said, 'Well, I don't know, we weren't taught about this in my days at medical school, but I will consult a chum of mine who's a leading psychiatrist.'

In due course, the report came back that I was quite obviously homosexual and what did I want to do about it? The doctor said if I wanted to change I could go and have this electro-therapy, reversion therapy. So I thought to myself, 'Well it doesn't sound much fun but I'll go and see what happens.' So I went off to Bristol, to this hospital where this chap explained to me that he would present pictures of attractive young men and if I suddenly got sexually aroused I should be given an electric shock, which would hopefully turn me off. Gradually he would substitute for the handsome young men, nubile ladies.

Well, he started off by showing me a lot of brunette moustachioed

164

Latins and I was really rather more attracted to sort of blond Nords, so it didn't sort of work very well. I didn't have a shock and I thought, 'I really can't do this, this is ridiculous.' So he said, 'You have to come clean, at least you have to reconcile with the fact that you are gay and I advise you to organize your life so that you can get sexual satisfaction in your own way, but without upsetting anybody. Don't under any circumstances tell your wife.'

And so I thought about it and thought, 'Well that's not going to be much fun for the rest of my life living a sort of hypocritical life, pretending to be one thing and not being that.' So I went straight back and told her.

She was sitting in the drawing-room and I went up to her and I said, 'Um, I've just been to see Ken, the doctor. He tells me I'm like X and Y.' And I mentioned these two gay friends down the road and she looked at me in absolute horror and I said, 'You do realize don't you that it doesn't really make one atom of difference to my affection for you, that it's something we have got to accept and come to an agreement and an arrangement about.'

She was extremely upset, as you could imagine. I told her that if she wanted to end the marriage and have a proper full marriage and children and so on, well we'd arrange a divorce. And she said 'No, absolutely not, I'm very fond of you.' She burst into tears and she asked was it anything she'd done, was it her fault, could she have done something differently?

It was far tougher on her than it was on me, don't get any wrong ideas about that because she immediately blamed herself. She thought that because she hadn't been feminine enough I had been sort of turned off her.

We remained married for another fifteen years. In the meantime I got a job in London and spent the week in London, living an entirely gay life. Then I had the weekends in the country with her and we lived like that for very many years.

Living as we were, in a fairly small community in the country, being fairly active in the local society, suddenly for somebody who appeared as a perfectly straightforward normal married couple, for it to be discovered that I was gay ... I had been farming and living in the country like a country squire if you like, and that all came to an end. I know for a fact that people gossiped about me, it was inevitable that they should, because I made very little effort to hide the fact that

I was gay. I'm sure people did gossip and this of course was very distressful from my wife's point of view. I just disregarded it, I couldn't care two hoots. They weren't part of my life in the sense that my London life became my basic life.

Nobody had the bad manners to come and say, 'Oh you're an old poofter.' If they had I would have probably kicked them in the arse, but they didn't.

Frank Davies

•

After his experiences as a Japanese prisoner of war Frank returned to England 'feeling like a freak.' He had lost all confidence in his appearance, and believed that he had no chance of finding a girlfriend. Joan worked in the Metro-Vickers factory where she was known as 'The Body' amongst the lads. Frank fell for her but thought she was too good-looking for him. Frank and Joan married in 1949 and still live happily together.

•

I thought, you know, 'what's me chances of getting married?' The prospects of finding a girl who wanted to settle down with someone who looked like me was pretty remote. I felt like a complete failure. Me mates saw the difference 'cos before I was a bit cocky, full of it, always in the thick of things. When I came back I was very subdued. It'd been a blow to your confidence, summat had gone. You felt that you'd been robbed of your manhood, that something had been taken away from you. You kind of couldn't stand up for yourself.

I worked in a factory and the office girls used to pass and there was some nice bonny girls. I used to look at them but I always used to feel they were looking at me out of pity. You know, I was still taking these pills to kill the malaria so I were still this yellow colour and I was trying to get meself into shape.

Joan worked in the offices upstairs and she used to have to walk through the factory every now and then to collect messages for her boss or something. She was a glamour piece, you know.

I'm working on this end bench and I'd seen her pass a few times. I could tell she was coming because you'd hear the other men further up. They used to bang their bench with a hammer and whistle you know, 'Hiya love, how about a date?' All this stuff and so I had a warning that she was on her way and I used to pretend that I wasn't interested. Occasionally her eyes 'ud meet me and I'd think, 'Oh, she keeps looking at me.' Then me mate mentioned it, he said, 'She's looking at you.'

'No, give over,' I says, 'There's plenty of young 'andsome fellas up and down 'ere, you're kidding.' I didn't think there was any way she could be interested in me. I still felt like a freak.

Gradually I got the courage up and one day while she was passing I made an excuse to get up. 'Oh excuse me,' I says. 'You look very nice today.' Something daft like that, start the coversation and ask her for a date. I was amazed when she said, 'Yes.' So we fixed it up there and then. I'd fallen, that was it, soon as our eyes met. Everything seemed to fit into place, it was just one of those natural things.

We went to the pictures, first night, held hands, bag of toffees, the usual stuff, little cuddle and away we went. That was the start. But I still had this nagging feeling that she was doing it out of pity, feeling sorry for a poor lad that had just come back from doing his bit. I could never believe it, you know, in the state I was in then. I couldn't believe that she really fancied me. I thought she was just playing me along, probably had two or three on the run. I couldn't believe that my luck was in because I had no confidence.

But then she seemed as keen on me as I was on her and she used to say I looked like Charles Boyer. He was her hero on the films. That boosted me ego a bit, lifted me spirits and from then on, that was it, madly in love, the pair of us.

She used to complain that I wasn't very demonstrative. You do all the rest of it, the cuddling and the snogging, but she used to keep saying, 'Do you love me?' And I'd say, 'Of course I do.' But she wanted me to say it and I used to say, 'Well, what's the difference, I'm proving it, I'm showing it. I don't go with anybody else, I'm faithful, loyal, what more d'you want? We've got a bank book we put money in together.' We'd have these kind of arguments. Then now and again I'd blurt it out like, when I'd had a drink.

You were smooching and you'd do all the usual, as near as you could and all this kind of stuff and get pushed away. You'd get put in yer place quite often. I mean, it wasn't for the want of trying, I was eager to get down to business but the women like have these different ideas.

Frank and Joan Davies at their wedding in 1949.

•

We were walking along and I think we were doing some window-shopping, we were looking at rings. I'd made me mind up and so I thought I'd ask her. I said, 'Which one d'you fancy there?' And it kind of came out like this. 'D'you think we should get married?' I put it like that so I didn't have to kind of lose face. She said, 'What d'you think I'm hanging here for?' And that was it. That was the engagement. I got the ring and then we still carried on saving, mind you, we hadn't enough you know to buy a house straightaway.

Anyway once we were engaged, of course, you'd thrown your hat in the ring. You'd committed yourself, so things were a lot easier. We used to go finding nice lonely spots round country walks and places like that, go to a nice little pub, have a few drinks, stroll along the towpath, and that was it. You had to choose yer places, you had to go for these long walks through the long grass in the meadows you know. Find places like that, opportunities. There was nothing like, 'Your place or mine?'

And contraception was hit and miss. It was up to the man, all very primitive stuff. You used to go for a haircut, you know, a trim, and the barber, knowing you were courting, he'd say, 'Anything for tonight, Sir?' At first I thought, 'What's he on about?' Then it clicked, you know. So it became a regular calling shop, a haircut and something for tonight Sir.

It was a very small wedding. We just couldn't afford it after we'd paid all out on the house. I think the thing that attracted me was that she was very caring, you know, sensitive and homely. I felt I didn't want anybody who could kind of put me down or give me a rough time, verbally. She had this lovely easy to get on with attitude. All the attributes that make a good wife and mother. So the first attraction was the glamorous part of it and the other happened to be a bonus.

CHAPTER SIX

The Father

———————— • ————————

In 1924 Alfred Jenkins, a tinworker in North Wales, became a father for the first time: 'I spent most of my time at the bottom of the stairs listening to my wife's agony. I could tell the pain she was in because she would shout out now and again. I was so distraught that I fainted there and then, I came round some hours after. I was presented with this lovely little baby and I remember the feelings of elation.'

For Alfred, like most men of his generation, childbirth was a mysterious and frightening event at which he had no desire to be present. During the first half of the century fathers were largely excluded from the birth of their children – it was seen as an exclusively female preserve. Most women did not want their husbands to see them in labour. At home they were kept well away by the midwife or doctor. Hospitals did not allow them in on births either. The medical orthodoxy was that they would be a nuisance, an embarrassment and a hygiene risk. The absence of the father at the birth set the pattern for a distant parental role in which they had precious little involvement in bringing up their children. This was an era when many dads were virtual strangers to their sons and daughters.

Fathers took little part in baby care. Many were terrified of holding small babies, fearing they might drop or harm them. The childcare manuals of the time reinforced these fears claiming that looking after infants was the natural domain of the mother alone. Interestingly, most of these manuals – like those of bestselling baby expert Dr Truby King – were written by men. Deep in the psyche of many men of this generation was a fear that helping with the baby would somehow undermine their masculinity. Few changed nappies. And even fewer were brave enough to be seen out pushing a pram.

Mike Walters was an office worker in Bristol in the 1930s. 'I had very little to do with John when he was a baby. I know I never changed his nappy. I was frightened he'd roll off the table or that I'd hurt him in some way. I never bathed him either, I think I was fright-

Alfred Jenkins and his wife Lillian shortly after their marriage in 1923.
They went on to have two sons and a daughter.

•

ened that he might drown. And the idea of a man pushing a pram, that was almost unheard of. I remember once saying, "I'm not going to push that bloody pram." I think that was embarrassment, everything to do with babies seemed to be embarrassing for men to get involved in.'

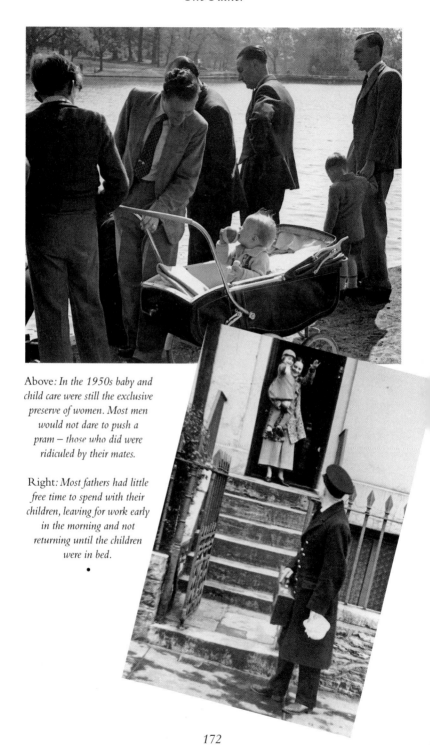

Above: *In the 1950s baby and child care were still the exclusive preserve of women. Most men would not dare to push a pram – those who did were ridiculed by their mates.*

Right: *Most fathers had little free time to spend with their children, leaving for work early in the morning and not returning until the children were in bed.*

•

Men who began to develop a liking for baby care were ridiculed as effeminate. In Lancashire men who pushed prams were known as 'Mary-Annes'. Frank Davies, a father devoted to caring for his baby daughter in Salford in the late 1940s, was very unusual in his open defiance of these kinds of taunts from friends and family. To avoid losing face, those who enjoyed helping with their babies often tried to keep it hidden from the outside world. Women were sometimes as keen as their husbands to keep the secret lest people assume they were not doing their jobs as mothers properly.

Leonard Small was a church minister in Bathgate near Edinburgh in the 1930s: 'I loved helping with the babies. I would often bath them and I must have walked miles holding them on my shoulder, patting their little backs, winding them. My wife never objected to me helping at home but she did to anyone seeing me doing anything with the babies. Once we were going up a steep hill and I was pushing the pram. That was fine until some women neighbours started walking towards us. She slapped my hand and said, "Take your hands off, you big Jessie".'

Though on the whole a distant figure, father was expected to be an emotional rock in dealing with the dangers that surrounded childbirth and childcare during the first decades of the century. Inadequate medical provision and the prevalence of infectious diseases meant that there were serious risks to the lives of mother and child. In the 1900s there was an annual death toll of 25 000 babies during birth or within the first four weeks of being born. And each year around 3 000 mothers lost their lives giving birth. Then there was a host of potentially fatal childhood diseases like whooping cough, diphtheria and scarlet fever. Medical improvements and immunization over the decades gradually reduced the numbers of these family tragedies but the convention that a man should always be in control of his emotions when dealing with them remained firmly entrenched. For Glyn Davies, a policeman in Sheffield just after the last war, the pressure to deal with the death of his newborn baby daughter in a manly way and his inability to express deep-seated emotions of loss and grief led to a nervous breakdown.

The father's most important role was that of provider. As the main breadwinner it was assumed he should not be expected to help much, if at all, with looking after the children when he came home tired from work. Those who commuted long distances or who

A trawlerman returns home after a three week stint at sea in 1942.

•

worked long hours or shifts had no choice. Few absent fathers that we interviewed questioned this role or felt they had missed out on anything important. Dave Bowman was an engine driver in Dundee in the 1940s with two small children:

•

If I were on night shift I slept during the day. If I woke up I'd some-times say, 'Stop these bloody kids shouting, I've got to get some sleep.' So you'd got no contact. If I were on the back shift and working quite a bit of overtime it's possible I wouldn't see the kids for a whole week, that's why my wife took charge of the kids, that's why I gave her the pay packet. This was because I was outside, I was the fellow who was doing the work, I was bringing in the money, so she must be the orga-nizer for the family. I accepted that, that was it.

•

So little time was spent with the children that many fathers of this generation have few memories of what they actually did with them. They recall some of the ritual activities of family life like Christmas – when they might proudly buy the children's presents – and summer holidays. But the main landmarks of a son or daughter's development – learning to walk, the first day at school, birthdays, and so on – so vividly remembered by mothers, simply passed most fathers by. Sometimes the father who worked very long hours or who was away for weeks at a time was such a distant figure, his relationship with his children was virtually non-existent. This problem was made worse during the last war which took millions of fathers away from home for periods of up to six years. On home leave, and when the war was over, some were seen by their children as total strangers. Geordie Todd remembers how painful and upsetting it was when his son refused to have anything to do with him after his return from war service.

The distance between father and child was also heightened by the part fathers played in imposing discipline in the home. One of the main concerns of parents continued to be with the control of their children and instilling obedience, good manners and respect for elders, as illustrated in the memories of Richard Nesbitt, a middle-class father with two boys in Exmouth in the post-war years. Usually it was the mother, responsible for most day-to-day discipline, who inflicted any punishment on the children. Father generally got involved in more serious offences on a 'wait till your father gets home' basis. Ray Rochford was a father in Salford in the late 1940s: 'I'd get in from work and my wife would tell me a list of things to deal with: "Michael's broken a window. Paul keeps spitting at me", and you'd have to dish out the punishments. You'd talk about it to your mates at work, "I had to give our Brian one last night y'know." It was like a Shakespearean part you played, Dad was the bad guy.'

Punishments ranged from smacked bottoms to more serious assaults. This was an era when the physical punishment of children was an accepted part of everyday life. Sons were more likely to be hit at home than daughters – this was one of the disadvantages of being a boy and being seen as stronger than your sisters. Harold Smith, brought up in Manchester in the twenties and thirties, chillingly describes living in fear of the unpredictable and extremely violent moods of his father who was disabled and badly traumatized during the First World War.

A few fathers refused to use any physical force whatsoever on their children, preferring persuasion to punishment. Often this was determined by individual personality and choice but there were also some regional and occupational variations in parental attitudes. There was, for example, a traditional disapproval of corporal punishment on the Shetland Islands. And in the Durham mining village of Chopwell – known locally as Red Chopwell – there were similar liberal attitudes towards children. Here a mix of high male unemployment, radical politics and libertarian ideals produced an atmosphere where alternative parenting could thrive. It is vividly remembered by George Short, an unemployed father with two children in the Depression years.

Much more typical of the parental attitudes of the age was the concern of many fathers to teach their sons to box. This was seen as an essential part of their training in manliness and also a way of helping them to survive on the streets and at school where the pecking order amongst boys was very much based on the ability to fight. What is most extraordinary is how young many boys were when Dad presented them with their first pair of boxing gloves. Bert Barnes, an electrician in Harlesden, North London, in the 1930s recalls: 'On my son's sixth birthday I bought him a set of four-ounce boxing gloves and we used to have sessions in the back garden. I used to put a set of eight-ounce gloves on and we used to spar.'

Fathers took great pride in the physical strength and courage of

Bert Barnes and his son John boxing in the back garden.
Bert bought John his first pair of boxing gloves
when he was only six years old.

their sons, who in turn were often desperate to please them by winning fights. Joe Phillips, brought up in the South Wales mining village of Senghenydd in the 1930s, remembers the humiliation of losing in front of his father: 'I was involved in this one fight, the boys formed a circle and this fellow started hammering me. I was bleeding in the nose, I was bleeding in the mouth, so I decided I had enough, so I quit. It wasn't an honourable thing to do and it was at that period when I stopped, much to my shame, I saw my father standing there and he just walked away. He didn't reckon on having sons to be quitters, no. I would have given my life to have carried on fighting but it was too late. All the hurt I had off the other chap disappeared because I was more hurt because my father walked away.'

Perhaps the most important activity that brought fathers and sons together was a shared interest in sport. Fathers of the pre-war years often recall with great fondness teaching their sons how to play football and cricket or going to matches together. It was through his son's desire to swim that Geordie Todd managed to re-establish a relationship with him after years of virtual silence. Many got closer to their sons as they grew older – a closeness that was often strengthened when the boy began work and started sharing a more adult social life with his father in pubs, clubs and sports teams. But the lasting impression of the fathers of this generation is how little they had to do with bringing up their children.

George Short

•

George was a gentle, dignified man with twinkling eyes. He had lived with his daughter Doris since his wife died. The family was very close, the love and respect between father and daughter was plainly obvious. George's eyes lit up whenever Doris came into the room. Sitting in his favourite rocking chair, George talked animatedly as he remembered his early days as a father, speaking in his lilting County Durham accent. Unemployed for most of the 1930s, socialist politics and the struggle for work were of central importance to him. It was with these values in mind that he raised his children. George died at the end of 1994 at the age of ninety-four.

•

George Short in his thirties while he was unemployed. He was a very idealistic father, keen to educate his children and give them an understanding of politics.

•

We never had anything in the shape of cane or anything. Most houses had a set of taws, a strip of leather split into little ribbons. We never had that and would have been horrified at the idea of our kids being hit with anything like that.

I didn't believe in corporal punishment either for them or for any other children. I tried to convince them and I thought that was the best way for them to learn, by the art of self-discipline. The way we were taught self-discipline was by the cane and I realized it was a failure. If I could convince my own children then

179

sure as anything they would respect my point of view, they would respect what I believed in and it paid off. I always made them try to understand that as they grew up they would never get anything for nothing, everything they had had to be fought for. I didn't believe that they could ever progress in life itself by climbing over other people, but that they and the class they came from, was dependent on the unity of those people.

Punishment was quite a problem and it meant you had to work a little bit harder because kiddies, it doesn't matter who they are, bairns are liable to get into trouble. But it paid off in the long run.

We never spoke a harsh word in front of the bairns, and the result would be that if we said jointly that something was bad and they shouldn't do it, that was like the law of the land with them.

I taught my children first of all the importance of education and taught them how to read and how to write. When they got to eight or nine we read *Oliver Twist*, Jack London, and all the Dickens stories. I always liked Dickens. Those that were on the side of the poor people always come out on top. No villains ever came out on top in Dickens' stories. I gave them a desire to learn to read and I always remembered how my old grandfather had taught me.

I enjoyed their company as kiddies and played about with them and taught them both how to swim in the River Derwent where there was a fairly deep pool.

Doris and Bill and their mother and I always went out at the weekends if we could. We went camping together, we went all over walking because where we lived you were surrounded by woodlands and we knew every inch of those woods. We wandered around that countryside to our hearts' content and the bairns used to enjoy going for walks with us.

Provided you weren't going poaching, nobody interfered with you and in the woods of course there was every form of wild animal. Rabbits used to run almost tame, and not only rabbits but hares. Then crawling about you'd find hedgehogs and things like that, so we would stop and look at these and, although I was never an authority on birds, I tried to encourage the children to get books which would tell them which birds were which.

You had to be very careful about lighting fires and I was always very cautious about that. But if we got into a place which was wide and I thought we could light a fire without any danger then the

George Short's daughter Doris and his son George
outside their home in Chopwell in the early 1930s.

•

bairns were sent to go and get some sticks and maybe some dry leaves and I would always take plenty of paper with me and we'd make a fire, not because we needed a fire but you know the idea of a fire when you're camping. And then Mother would always take with her a load of food and we would have a good picnic.

We had nothing as elaborate as a bell tent or anything like that so what we tended to do it was more to fire the imagination of the youngsters about camping. We used our own type of tent, you know, a lump of canvas stretched over crossed sticks just so that the bairns got the imagination of camping but then at night we would fold our tent up and then we would go back home.

Doris was my eldest daughter and her mother was a big influence on her. But sometimes I would talk to her and I would tell her about the sort of life that we had lived when we were younger, about the life that our parents and their parents before them had lived. Therefore Doris and I became very close because she sort of appreciated and understood this approach. So then I used to take her out with me and when I used to speak for the unemployed, when she was very little, she would come with me down to Stockton Cross and sit on there while I spoke for the unemployed.

I never believed in this idea of flag-waving and so on either and I was determined that my kiddies wouldn't be indoctrinated with this sort of rubbish either. When we lived at Chopwell and they were very young we went to the school and brought 'em out on Empire Day and wouldn't let the kiddies take part in the celebrations. I regarded it all as false patriotism. I've always tried to make the children feel that they shouldn't get involved in waving the Union Jack, singing 'God Save the King', or 'God Save the Queen'. If God wants to save the King and save the Queen that's his business, it's not ours, and they're not as much in need of being saved as what we are.

I always taught our Doris that she must stick up for herself and she mustn't let anybody put on to her, nor must she ever let anybody put on to Bill. She used to fight like a lad you know, she didn't fight like a lass, pulling hair and things like that, she used to punch and of course she got as good as what she sent sometimes. I always remember this time when she came in and whoever she'd been fighting with had clouted her on the nose and made her nose bleed and she had started to cry and rubbed the tears and blood all over her face. She was like a Red Indian when she came in and 'Oh my God, what have you been up to now?' The thing was that she wasn't bothered about whether she'd got hurt or not, the most important thing she wanted to impress on me was that she'd her own back first.

She won a scholarship at Norton and it was right during the period when her mother and I had been arrested for demonstrating for the unemployed and I was sent to gaol. Well somebody had made some derogatory remarks about me being in prison and she whipped around and clouted them. At first the reaction of the people at the school was that they should expel her because girls weren't supposed to fight like that. But after they got to know why it had happened they let it drop. It really made me feel proud that if anybody had anything to say either about me, her mother, or her brothers, then they would have her to deal with.

Harold Smith

•

Harold lives with his wife Carol in a small cottage outside Bradford-on-Avon in Wiltshire. His health is not good. He is a gentle man, very emotional but proud. An Oxford education and a short career in the diplomatic service have not rid his voice of its Mancunian roots. He was born in Manchester in 1927, the fifth child of Harry and Maggie Smith. His father, a shirtcutter, had served as an infantryman with the Manchester Regiment during the First World War. His father's experiences in the front line deeply affected the way he raised his children, so much so that Harold describes himself as a victim of the war 'almost as much as if I had been in the trenches myself'.

•

We knew that the war meant a lot to my father because, although he didn't talk about it, his friends talked about him and his experiences, that he'd been a hero. His values all seemed to spring from the trenches. 'He's a good man to have in a trench, he'd never let you down, he'd never run, he'd stand his ground.' He'd greet his friends and say, 'Up the box, up the box lads, up the box.' This reference to this secret background in the trenches.

He couldn't bear to think of all his friends, he used to call it the bloody butcher's shop – bits of bodies everywhere, all your friends torn to pieces. So that was a very important element in my upbringing because I felt that my dad's violence towards me was because somehow he wanted the new generation to be like all his friends who'd died. He didn't want us to let them down, we had something to live up to.

We felt different because my father only had one leg and one eye, and suffered. Sometimes when he'd been drinking it was very dangerous to be around because he would take out his feelings on anybody. But the next day he'd have no recollection whatsoever about what had happened. My mother found the drinking hard to live with so she did what a lot of wives did, she joined him and she got hooked too.

It's crazy to think that my father was drinking because of me but I felt I was doing something wrong, I didn't know what I was doing wrong and it was quite a long time before I realized it had nothing to do with me. I was just part of the furniture of his life.

It was so strange because as a morning person he was quite normal, but once he'd been drinking he was a different person and eye-to-eye contact was very dangerous. 'Who're you looking at? Look at me, look at me. Stand up when I speak to you.' And suddenly the fist, repeated blows, being kicked around.

I felt that part of the beating up was to make you cry and to humiliate you and to break you down and to make you nothing, so that you were destroyed. If you could hold on to something you could get through it. I remember the actual occasion that I wouldn't cry, I knew that I couldn't go on living like that and I wanted him to kill me rather than go on being beaten. When I was about nine or ten I stood up and said, 'Hit me but I won't cry'. He raised his hand and he couldn't do it and then he was impressed by this and then he began to say that his son, his lad, was going to be a bloody good boy, he'd got the gift, he could talk and I was going to be a lawyer.

I was really being brought up to be a boy soldier. He expected me to go out and fight and show him that I was tough and I wasn't like that at all. Sometimes they would be there, my mother and father, and they would watch me. It had to be somebody much bigger than myself and all my instincts were to run but he would never, ever, allow that. I remember one boy saying to me, 'Oh, this is crazy, I'm just fed up of hitting you because you're a lousy fighter'. I was humiliated, I hated it and I would go to him, my father, and he'd turn away and say, 'You weren't much good'.

My father taught me that it was only your self-respect and pride that mattered and that it didn't matter at all what anybody else said about you. He talked about being a gentleman and he said that being a gentleman was the way you behaved and the way you thought of yourself. You didn't have to have any money to be a gentleman. This seems to jar with what I'm saying about the violence but it co-existed. He was very, very keen on cleanliness and standing up and cleaning your shoes and being respectful. And ladies had to be treated properly. It was important to open doors for them, offer them your seat and generally behave with them like a little gentleman should.

He never demonstrated affection by holding you or touching you. We were a non-touching family and that was it. He didn't like it and he disapproved of showing one's emotions. Although he sobbed in the night he hated to be seen so I would try to find out from him

Harold Smith's father Harry, before he joined the Manchester Regiment as an infantryman in 1914.

•

about the war and what happened. But each time he attempted to explain he would bury his head in his hands and he would sob, especially if you mentioned his friends and he'd just say, 'All gone, all gone'. My mother would say, 'Leave him alone, don't talk about the war.' But, of course, I was curious to have him talk about it. I think he felt if you cried you weren't being brave and that's not the way a man had to behave.

One way that he showed me affection was when I was ill and I was often ill as a child. I had these terrible fevers and it was very difficult to see a doctor in the thirties, you had to pay. He had his own primitive ideas on medicine, like the red flannel round your neck for colds or an old sock round your neck if you had a bad throat. He told me that in the trenches, for trench foot you peed on your feet. When I had the fevers he would carry me into his bed and he would hold me very tight, he would put me in one of his nightshirts, his flannel shirts which he'd made himself, and I loved that. I loved to be with my dad, you see I loved him dearly, and to be put into one of his flannel nightshirts. He'd be covered in sweat too and then, it was on these occasions that I would sleep and come out of the fever.

So you see if my father was sobbing I would comfort him and there was a kind of role reversal. Those terrible nightmares he used to have. You don't know what the hell went on there, you just know he's having a really rough time and you understand him, why he drinks, although I hated it. He couldn't bear to be sober because when he was sober he wanted to talk about what happened and he couldn't talk about what happened. He had a lot of pain and so that we tended to feel as children that we were carers. He drank a lot because he had the terrible nightmares and he would scream in the night.

I think he was stunted himself. I think the searing, the burning experience that he'd had had stopped his living, I think he stopped in those trenches. The youthful ideals that he had, and he must have been a very good man, it all stopped.

Geordie Todd

•

Geordie lives alone in North Shields in the flat where he and his wife Ellen raised their only son Peter, who was born in 1938. Surrounded by family photographs, Geordie occupies his time doing jigsaw puzzles, many of which are framed on the walls. His work as a fisherman meant long periods away from home, so he had little time to spend with his son as he was growing up. The Second War World meant he missed out on even more of Peter's childhood. Geordie was three years without home leave. He remembers his victory homecoming with a tinge of sadness. Peter would have nothing to do with him and he had to struggle to win back his son's affections. Peter died in 1980.

•

We'd been married three year when Peter was born, an eight-month baby, three pounds in weight. I was quite happy that I wasn't in at the birth 'cos I believe she had a bad time and I would

Geordie Todd and his son Peter in the back yard of their home in North Shields.
A few months later Geordie was sent overseas with the naval convoys.

•

have hated to see her suffering. I was quite pleased to arrive after it was all finished.

I came in from sea, it was thick fog and of course ya come up the river quite quietly and gently and when we passed Lloyds Sailing Station the hailer shouted through the megaphone, 'What ship? *Donovan, John Donovan?* That you George? You got a little lad and the orders are you got to go up straightaway to the hospital'. I was that much delighted I gave the crew the price of a drink each.

She must have been yelling my name out during the delivery and when I walked down the ward the wife looked up and she's waving from her bed. I can remember as if it was yesterday and all the women on each side of the ward were saying, 'Oh, this must be

George'. Well, my face, God, it must have went crimson.

He was in an incubator with him being so small but he sharp grew after we brought him home. You would see a difference every time I came in from sea.

We spent as much time as we could together but I was away fishing for days, maybe weeks at a time. I had a job to do for to keep me wife and new family the way I wanted to therefore I had to go to sea more and work harder. As long as me son and me wife was well cared for, well provided for, I didn't care what hours I put in, as long as I knew they were all right. Mind, she worried about me. I provided for the wife well and as me son grew you know the wife was always buying this for him and that for him. I think it was two or three tricycles he had and in no time then he had his pedal car. I brought that all the way from Edinburgh and I even sat in the guard's van with it to make sure nobody pinched it.

I don't think he was quite three year old when I was called up for service and when I came home from abroad he was six or seven and he didn't know me, he didn't recognize me. At first, when he saw us on Newcastle Station he was shouting, 'Which is me dad?' The son didn't want to have anything to do with us when I arrived back. When we came home that night we went to bed and he came into our room and put the light on and he says, 'You, out , that's my mam's bed, not yours, out'. And that sort of upset us. I said, 'Well I'm yer dad, I'm supposed to stay here.' He couldn't get it and at the finish we had to bring him in between us. He thought I was an interloper, I was coming in between him and his mam and he couldn't see why I should, 'cos he had been with his mother all these years. It grieved me terrible.

During the time I was on leave for a month he hardly ever spoke to us and anything he wanted me to buy him came through the wife. When he used to come from school, if I was at home he used to say, 'Ask me dad for this, ask me dad for that.'

I felt very awful. Even when I'd been demobbed it was still going on. 'Course, I went back to the fishing. I used to come in the house from a fishing trip and I used to put me bag away, me fish and that, and speak to the wife, give her a cuddle and a kiss and he would sit there. He would never say, 'Hello Dad'. Nothing. Many a time I felt like getting hold of him and giving him a damn good shake, but I refrained from that. I didn't want to start badly using him in any way.

Me own father had treated me like that and I knew how that felt. I wanted to be different with me own. So I thought to meself, 'Give him time and he'll come round.'

Many a time I felt as if I could have like half murdered him and when I got to that stage I used to just put me coat on and go out and have a pint. Of course the wife knew what was happening and she knew I was going through hell.

We loved each other very, very much, the wife and I, but I felt that we weren't a family, not as I thought we should be, three together. I was getting a bit depressed about it. You come in and you're flogged inside out, you've washed about the North Sea, you've done all sorts and when you come in your son just walks past you as if you aren't there. To me I couldn't grasp that at all, to me that wasn't family.

Anyway he knew I was a good swimmer and by this time he was about nine or ten, summat like that, and he was dying to swim. He came in from school one day and he says to his mam, he says, 'Would you ask me dad to teach us to swim?' And she says, 'If you want to swim you ask your dad. I've asked him for too much already, time you asked him.' I was sitting there and he came through and he asked me. So of course I did teach him, started the next day. I used to teach him on a stool in the house first and as the time went on he became a very good swimmer. I taught him just the crawl and he was entered in the gala, took his bronze medal, and then his silver medal.

It made all the difference between him and I. It was always Dad this and Dad that after that. We became very, very close after, him and I was great.

I came in from sea and when he came from school, it was, 'You want a swim?' We'd go and have a swim. I used to give him half a length for a start. Then as the months and years went on we cut the start down. I think he was about fifteen and one day he said, 'Come on then Dad, straight start'. The wife started us, both together, and away we went and I beat him, only just. To tell you the truth I was buggered. He says, 'Come on Dad, again.' But I says, 'No way. Yer dad's a champion and he's going to retire as champion'.

As the months went on he hung on to me more and more, as a son should to his dad and I was appreciating it. Then when I was going fishing he was wanting to go too. He was starting his summer break and so I took him with me. I said, 'Mind, if it's bad weather there's no coming back. You just got to be sick and put up with it. Once we go

Geordie Todd and Peter (left).
Geordie was away from his family for six years during the war.
The fishing trips with his son brought them closer together again.

•

out there you're out there till the trip's finished.' All he was interested
in was picking all the bits of debris and the likes of that up, shells and
that. We had a goldfish tank on the window-sill, thirty gallons of
water in it, and he wanted to save the shells that we were picking up
in the net for to make arches for the fish to swim through.

I wouldn't let him move about the deck during the dark, that was
taboo, soon as it became dusk – 'Good night' and in the bunk. We
used to talk about all different things and once he talked about when
I was in the Service, which he had never ever asked about before. It
became a ritual, every night when I made him go to bed I used to tell

some of my experiences. I felt really a dad again, like being a real father.

The following year he wanted to come again but this time he split his fingers. On the boat you had a big sharpening stone, sandstone, oh about eighteen inches long by about six inches wide and two or three inches thick, where you kept your knives nice and sharp for mending the nets. I was mending a net and asking him to pass the stone over to where we were working and of course when he plonked the stone down he forgot to take his fingers from underneath it and busted his fingers. The next year he was running along the deck – which we impress on everybody never run on the deck – and he turns round, bumped straight into a pole and his eye's up like that, every colour in the rainbow. When we comes in, he marches in and his mam sees him, she says, "What you trying to do, kill him?'

When he came in and saw his pals and said, 'Oh I've been to sea with me dad, me dad's a skipper.' He was boasting sort of style, and of course that made me feel better again.

Richard Nesbitt

•

Since he was widowed he has lived alone in a beautiful town house in Arlesford, Hampshire, which he inherited from his mother. Very upright, and smartly dressed, he speaks with a Scottish burr which comes from his grandmother who he lived with for long periods as a child. After working in Navy Intelligence during the Second World War he spent twenty years in charge of management training for Shell in the West Country. At eighty-four he is still very busy with various committees. He has a West Highland terrier for company. He married Esmé in 1944 and they had two sons, born in 1946 and 1949.

•

The sister came and told me it was a son. Esmé had had a rough time and she was very exhausted and so I only stayed a few minutes, but I was tickled pink. Here was a great big bouncing boy. I was very dishevelled, of course, I hadn't had much sleep that night and went off to this party of a very old friend of mine who had just announced his engagement. I should have been ashamed to turn up in such a dishevelled way but I didn't give a hoot, drank as much champagne as I could.

John's pattern was slightly different because after Esmé's experience of going up to the nursing home too early she was determined not to do it again. She held out at home until labour had started and that was very disconcerting. She then said, 'Drive me up there.'

I remember saying, 'Well, shall I drive slowly and avoid the bumps or shall I drive quickly but it'll be very bumpy?'

And she said, 'Drive as fast as you can and to hell with it.' Very shortly after we got to hospital John was born, there was no delay whatever, but I wasn't allowed near again until it was all over and done with.

I was away quite often working and so it was a great treat to have a long weekend at home and enjoy the family. In the summer the beach dominated, most particularly when John was small, but as they both got older and stronger, came the tricycle phase and that broadened horizons. He would go much farther than his legs would carry him. We used to go for walks along the banks of the Otter and picnic up there.

You always tried to stop them shouting in the house. It was bad enough that they shouted out in the garden, because it might upset the neighbours, but they did. But shouting in the house, no, they would be checked. They had a room upstairs where they could play and do what they liked, and they raised a good deal of noise up there. It was a question of behaviour, certain marks of respect which were clearly defined. Getting up when adults came in the room, opening doors for them, shaking hands and addressing them politely were others. If you could get them started along these lines it was a good beginning.

They shouldn't fill their mouths chock-a-block, they shouldn't push food over the table. Once they'd got the idea of a spoon and fork and then it was merely a question of keeping their food under control, not playing with it. I think those are the basic principles. If you could get them into civilized behaviour, the sooner the better.

Respect for parents or for adults was something we didn't teach as such. It was rather an outlook and attitude. If children are insolent and rude when adults are about you curb it, to check it and stop it. It was sowing seeds of thought and conditioning that otherwise wouldn't have occurred to them. Children don't behave well or nicely

*Richard Nesbitt and his sons Robert and John in the garden of
their family home in Devon.*

•

naturally, and I don't think you'll make them do so by telling them
what to do, it's rather what not to do.

It wasn't that they shouldn't ever cry, I think it was rather that having seen what a rough, tough world it was, they should be able to
face it. Life doesn't owe you a living, you've got to get out there and
get stuck in and make your own way. I don't think that either of
them were cry babies. I remember an occasion, John used to walk
about a lot with bare feet and he used to go into my workshop
where I often had odd things in there and he picked up a very heavy
condenser, about six inches long. He dropped it on his little toe and
the howl of agony that went up went straight to my heart, a cry of
despair. I picked him up and hugged him and hugged him. I did my
best to see that they were not mollycoddled and grew up as tough
youngsters and I think they are.

I don't know what went on during the week except I would hear if there had been trouble. By and large there was a threat, 'I'll tell Dad if you're not careful.' It was effective. I was the bogey-man who it wasn't wise to offend.

When I wasn't there on a normal day the children would be upstairs in their playroom and Esmé would be in the kitchen, but there was never any trouble. When I was at home sometimes they'd start fighting, raising Cain, well I'd stop the fighting and I'd stop their noise, had no trouble in doing so. I only had to growl at them if you like, and they would stop.

If John was in one of his moods he could easily find himself sent upstairs, and so on occasions, but not very often, he got a smack. And if it was a smack it was a good smack, on the bottom and he didn't forget it. That was the hierarchy of punishment but I always tried to ensure that they were very short and sharp and not dragged out.

A parent hopes to do as well, if not better, for his young than what he enjoyed. I wanted to give my boys a boarding-school education. I began to look around the West Country, Devon in particular and I visited, oh, most of the boarding-schools in the area and had a good look at them. There was one that remains in my memory, Dartington Hall, which even in those days was known as being very liberal. There were boys and girls, co-educational, so I looked with amazement at this. It never occurred to me that they were candidates for Dartington. Kelly College in Tavistock really stood out. It had a strong naval tradition, it was started by Admiral Kelly and he made a jolly good job of it so Rob went to Kelly, followed by John and it did them well.

I think both of them had a first term of homesickness and then settled down and took to it. It was built around the sports ground and no other schools, except public schools, had facilities to compare with this. It ensured that the boys were fully occupied from dawn to dusk, which keeps them out of mischief. They worked hard and they played hard and at the end of the day they had no energy. This was no bad pattern for the young to grow up in. Certain sports, rugger particularly, got rid of aggression and taught youngsters to take knocks that came their way. In a rugger scrum, oh boy, you do take knocks but they don't seem to do any lasting damage.

It gave them a self-sufficiency, self-confidence. Those were things that I certainly hoped for for my boys and I had to make a hell of a lot of sacrifice. Esmé and I, we both did. We sacrificed holidays and a lot of other things that we could have enjoyed otherwise to do so, but I never regret it. I was considered by most of my friends and colleagues to be well paid but it wasn't well enough to have two boys at public school and the bills. It got hard to struggle on but in retrospect I think it was worth it because there was no alternative at the time.

Glyn Davies

•

He was nervous of being interviewed. Quietly spoken, understated, even shy, you would not guess that he had been a policeman. Since his divorce Glyn has lived alone in Colwyn Bay. Now they live apart he and his wife get on better than ever and are the best of friends. Glyn is passionate about music and sings in a male voice choir. He married in 1946 and his only son, Alan, was born in 1948. He and his wife lost a daughter in 1956 when she was only a few minutes old.

•

M y wife was very anxious, and I was too, to have another child. I always wanted a little girl, and she became pregnant, she went every month to the clinic, and at the eighth month they kept her in because things had gone wrong. So she was kept in there for about six weeks, knowing that the child was dead inside. Then again she lost a baby within a short period of weeks and then the last pregnancy went to the full time. We were so pleased and we were looking forward to the birth. We were really thinking that this time it would all be okay.

I was on duty, on the evening shift, and when I came back home I could see something had gone wrong in the house by the atmosphere. My wife's father was walking about chomping his lips, he was very nervous and said, 'There's something I want you to know'. But I pushed him to one side and went straight to the bedroom. I was concerned more about the wife, never thought anything about the baby, never entered my head. She looked so dreadful, ashen and she started crying and we put our arms around each other. Then they told me that the child, a little girl, had died.

I found out that the baby had been put into a cloth in the next bedroom. I didn't tell her that, of course. Then everybody left us, my wife and myself, alone, and I was trying my best to comfort her. The next morning the funeral undertaker came and that was a very difficult part. The child had some clothing round it and they lifted it and put it in the coffin and I asked to see the face again. I can still see that little girl's face in that coffin to this day. She was very much like my wife, dark hair. I shall never forget that as long as I live, and even to this day when I look at children, at little girls, at the age which mine would have been, I do envy those people tremendously.

One struggled to try and keep face, you didn't want to show your emotions to anybody else and I didn't for years. I suppose you feel you've got to carry on like. It seems as though there's an unwritten law in our time 'Man mustn't cry, mustn't show his feelings'. I was never told by anybody you mustn't but there was something in the back always that if a man started crying there was whispering. 'What's up with him?' And I also felt that if I broke down it would upset my wife. If I couldn't hold the fort up what was she going to do. I felt if I walked about as if I'd got over it and everything's fine that she would improve. I felt if I crack, well, the whole lot cracks.

We went through a bad period at that time, the wife was very depressed and I was working long hours and trying to get as much money as possible. When you are on nights, you'd come off at seven in the morning, you were on duty again at twelve till six, anything to get more money you know. And I just cracked up, had a sort of a nervous breakdown. That's the reason why I had to leave the police force.

I know I lived through it but I can't remember a thing about it. You're living, you're actually with people, you can hear them, yet you're in a bubble, you're somehow detached from everybody. I could burst into tears at any time and I remember I used to walk from the bus back home and very often I've come as far as some steps leading to a farmyard and I'd sit on there and burst out crying. I didn't know why it was happening, why I was crying – me, a man, crying. Nothing happened that day, you didn't have a row and you didn't have a fight, nothing, you've just been to work. But it's just that the illness, the depression, makes you feel like that.

And when I got home I didn't feel like kissing or messing about at all. It's the last thing you want. All I wanted was to be left alone in peace. I felt completely inadequate because the sex side of a man is the most vulnerable part isn't it, and if you feel that you can't indulge your sex well that's the last thing, you're finished, you're no good to anybody. It's a dreadful feeling, frightening.

And you couldn't tell anybody you're like that at all or they would whisper, 'Oh, he's suffering with his nerves'. You don't tell anybody you've been to a psychiatrist or you feel you'll be cast out. There was a stigma about nervous illnesses, as if it's something contagious.

My doctor sent me to a psychiatrist and I had what is called ECT treatment, electrical convulsive treatment. And that made me snappy, irritable. And people at work can't understand what's wrong with

Glyn Davies with his son Alan.
Glyn joined the police force in Sheffield in 1946 and served for eight years.
•

you. 'What the devil's the matter with you?' But I just kept it to meself, didn't show any emotions at all. Well, what if you saw a policeman crying? You'd think he was mad wouldn't you? I'd got to do the job I was being paid for and I didn't want to disgrace meself.

But eventually it got to the time that I had to pack it up, I resigned. I wasn't doing the job properly, I felt I wasn't adequate to do the job, that I was weak.

I was still going every week for this treatment then, to be knocked out for four hours. I don't know how long I went, six weeks or something. But I arrived at the hospital one day and I was told to go to the doctor's office. And he said, 'You've been very ill you know.' And I said, 'Have I?' That's the first time that I realized how ill I had been.

Frank Davies

•

Frank and Joan lost their first child. Their daughter, Val, was born in 1953. They remain a very close family, and Val lives with them in the family home in Salford.

•

I wanted to be different to how me own father treated us. Well, I thought, well you know you're responsible for this new life. So I was determined to be the father, to do everything you know, everything that's expected of you. I wanted to be there and let them talk to me if they wanted to and listen to all the problems and do all that's necessary so that they can look upon me as a father, not as some remote man that brings money in every week.

Joan had a rough time actually when we had Val. It turned out she'd got this rhesus negative blood group and she was very ill for quite a few months in the first stages of pregnancy, sick every day, in and out of hospital, so it was a bit of a rough period.

I wasn't there for the actual birth. I never heard of any men that wanted to go and witness the birth of the babies, it was taboo. It'd have frightened us to death. But it was a great relief and a thrill like when Val was born. We were delighted we'd got a little daughter, so she was spoiled then.

I used to do all the nappies, nursing, feeding, whatever was

Above: *Frank Davies with his daughter Val in the back garden of their home in Salford, Manchester.*

Right: *Frank Davies and Val on the beach at Rhyl, North Wales, in the early 1960s.*

necessary, I did it. Take her out for long walks in the pram, give the wife time to kind of get the housework done or what she needed and I used to enjoy that. I used to walk for miles round here, pushing the old pram, 'She's mine'. You know.

People in the neighbourhood, you'd walk out and you'd see them, 'Huh, look at him, pushing a kid'. But it never used to worry me, that.

They used to look and say, 'What's up with Joan, is she ill?'

I'd say, 'No, she's just doing something, ironing, I'm taking the kid.'

'Oh, you wouldn't get me doing that.'

You know that was the general attitude, and I used to think, 'Well what the hell is it? She's my daughter, she's my flesh and blood, what's wrong with pushing her round in her pram?' I just couldn't weigh it up. I used to think, 'If they say anything I'll flatten 'em.' I used to think it was the right thing to do. These are your children and why not?

Well, even me brother, you know, he'd got two daughters like but he'd never done anything like that and when he saw me doing these things he used to say, 'Hey what are you doing? That's not your job, that's a woman's job'. I said, 'Well that's not the way I look at it, it's my kid, I'm just as much entitled to do this as anybody else.' We used to have rows.

When you'd done all yer chores or it was a nice quiet night, I'd say, 'I'll go down to the pub, you know, and have a pint and I'll bring you a bottle back.' It was a regular routine. I used to go and you'd see yer mates in there who you'd normally have a drink with. They'd expect you to be there for the night and I used to say, 'I can't stop I'm just having a pint and I'll get a bottle for Joan.' Well, they used to have a go at ya then. 'Oh, she's got you under her thumb, you don't reckon to do that. You're a right wimp you know.'

Their attitude was that as long as they earned the corn and gave the wife the money, the rest was up to her. Bring the kids up, do all that's necessary and they didn't want to know. All they wanted was to see the results. It used to really get to ya and I used to end up rowing with them. You'd end, packing yer mates in and they would put the word round that, 'Oh, ah, he's a bit that way, you know, bit of a jessie'.

Further Reading

Bourke, J. *Working Class Cultures in Britain 1890-1960*. Gender, Class and Ethnicity. Routledge, 1993

Bott, A. *Our Fathers: Manners and Customs of the Ancient Victorians 1870-1900*. Heinemann, 1981

Bristow, J. *Empire Boys*. HarperCollins, 1991

Brod, H (ed). *The Making of Masculinities. The New Men's Studies*. Allen and Unwin, 1987

Brown, M. *The Imperial War Museum Book of the Western Front*. Sidgwick and Jackson, 1993

Caplan, P (ed). *The Cultural Construction of Sexuality*. Routledge, 1990

Chapman, R. and Rutherford, J (eds). *Male Order: Unwrapping Masculinity*. Lawrence and Wishart, 1988

Corr, H. and Jamieson, L (eds). *The Politics of Everyday Life. Continuity and Change in Work, Labour and the Family*. Macmillan, 1990

Davies, A. *Leisure, Gender and Poverty. Working Class Culture in Salford and Manchester*, 1900-1939. Open University Press, 1992

Gillis, J.R. *For Better, For Worse. British Marriages 1600 to the Present*. Oxford University Press, 1988

Hall, L. *Hidden Anxieties. Male Sexuality 1900-1950*. Polity Press, 1991

Hearn, J. *Men in the Public Eye. The Construction and Deconstruction of Public Men and Public Patriarchies*. Routledge, 1992

Hendrick, H. *Images of Youth. Age, Class and the Male Youth Problem 1880-1920*. Clarendon, Oxford 1990

Heward, C. *Making a Man of Him. Parents and their Sons' Education at an English Public School 1929-1950*. Routledge, 1988

Hey, V. *Patriarchy and Pub Culture*. Tavistock, 1986

Humphries, S et al. *A Century of Childhood*. Sidgwick and Jackson, 1988

Humphries, S. *Hooligans or Rebels? An Oral History of Working-Class Childhood and Youth 1889-1939*. Blackwell, 1983

Humphries, S. *A Secret World of Sex. Forbidden Fruit - The British Experience 1900-*

1950. Sidgwick and Jackson, 1988

Humphries, S. and Gordon, P. *A Labour of Love. The Experience of Parenthood in Britian 1900-1950.* Sidgwick and Jackson, 1992

Humphries, S. and Gordon, P. *Forbidden Britain. Our Secret Past 1900-1960.* BBC Books, 1994

Jackson, A.A. *The Middle Classes 1900-1950.* David St John Thomas, 1992

Keegan, J. *The Face of Battle: Study of Agincourt, Waterloo and the Somme.* Pimlico, 1991

Keen, S. *Fire in the Belly: On Being a Man.* Piatkus, 1992

Kimmel, M. and Messner, M (eds). *Men's Lives.* Macmillan, Allyn and Bacon (US), 1995

Kuhn, A. *Cinema, Censorship and Sexuality, 1909-1925.* Routledge, London and New York, 1989

Leed, E. *No Man's Land. Combat and Identity in World War One.* Cambridge University Press, London and New York 1979

Mangan, J.A. *Athleticism in the Victorian and Edwardian Public School.* Cambridge University Press, 1981

Mangan, J.A. and Walvin, J. *Manliness and Morality. Middle Class Masculinity in Britian and America 1800-1940.* Manchester University Press, 1987

Mason, P. *The English Gentleman. The Rise and Fall of an Ideal.* Pimlico, 1993

Middleton, P. *The Inward Gaze. Masculinity and Subjectivity in Modern Culture.* Routledge, 1992

Morgan, D.H.J. *Discovering Men: Sociology and Masculinities - Critical Studies on Men and Masculinities.* Routledge, London and New York 1992

Polity Press. *The Polity Press in Gender Studies.* 1993

Segal, L. Slow Motion. *Changing Masculinities, Changing Men.* Virago Press Ltd, 1990

Seidler, V.J. *Rediscovering Masulinity. Reason, Language, and Sexuality.* Routledge, 1989

Thompson, P. *The Voice of the Past. Oral History.* Oxford University Press, 1988

Thompson, P. *The Edwardians. The Remaking of British Society.* Routledge, 1992

Index

─────────── • ───────────

Page references in **bold** denote photographs. Page numbers in *italics* denote personal testimony.

Picture Credits

BBC Books would like to thank the following for providing photographs and for permission to reproduce copyright material. While every effort has been made to trace and acknowledge all copyright holders, we would like to apologise should there have been any errors or omissions.